Rebel V

Róisín McBrinn is a theatre director. S̶ Clean Break in 2018. Prior to this she v̶ since 2014 with responsibility for commissioning and developing writers and artists. She has directed many productions including shows at The Abbey Theatre, The Gate Theatre (Dublin), West Yorkshire Playhouse, The Donmar Warehouse, Sheffield Theatres, The Bush Theatre and Sherman Theatre.

For Clean Break, she has directed *Joanne* by Deborah Bruce, Theresa Ikoko, Laura Lomas, Chinonyerem Odimba and Ursula Rani Sarma; *House* by Somalia Seaton; *Amongst the Reeds* by Chinonyerem Odimba; and *Thick as Thieves* by Katherine Chandler.

Lauren Mooney is a writer, producer and dramaturg. She joined Clean Break in 2016 and worked as their Literary Producer until autumn 2018, supporting emerging writers and producing the company's engagement work in prisons.

Since 2015, she has co-run Kandinsky Theatre Company with director James Yeatman, where her work as producer and co-writer includes *Dog Show*, *Still Ill* and *Trap Street* (all New Diorama Theatre). In 2019, the company's work will include *Dinomania* (New Diorama Theatre), *There Is A Light That Never Goes Out* (Royal Exchange Theatre, Manchester) and a transfer of 2018 show *Trap Street* to the Schaubühne am Lehniner Platz in Berlin. She is a graduate of the Royal Court Introduction to Playwriting course (2015) and has written extensively about theatre, arts and culture for *Exeunt*, *The Stage* and *The Guardian*. She is currently the David Higham Scholar on the Creative Writing MA at University of East Anglia.

Rebel Voices

Monologues for Women by Women

Celebrating 40 Years of Clean Break

Edited by

RÓISÍN MCBRINN AND LAUREN MOONEY

methuen | drama

LONDON • NEW YORK • OXFORD • NEW DELHI • SYDNEY

METHUEN DRAMA
Bloomsbury Publishing Plc
50 Bedford Square, London, WC1B 3DP, UK
1385 Broadway, New York, NY 10018, USA

BLOOMSBURY, METHUEN DRAMA and the Methuen Drama logo are
trademarks of Bloomsbury Publishing Plc

First published in Great Britain 2019

Copyright © Róisín McBrinn and Lauren Mooney, 2019

Róisín McBrinn and Lauren Mooney have asserted their right under the Copyright,
Designs and Patents Act, 1988, to be identified as editors of this work.

For legal purposes the Acknowledgements on pp. xii and 103–105 constitute an
extension of this copyright page.

Cover design by Louise Dugdale
Cover image: 'Thalassa' © Swoon Studio, with thanks

A catalogue record for this book is available from the British Library.

A catalog record for this book is available from the Library of Congress.

ISBN: PB: 978-1-350-09750-6
ePDF: 978-1-350-09752-0
eBook: 978-1-350-09751-3

Series: Audition Speeches

Typeset by Deanta Global Publishing Services, Chennai, India
Printed and bound in Great Britain

To find out more about our authors and books visit www.bloomsbury.com
and sign up for our newsletters.

*Dedicated to the memory of our dear friend and colleague
Helen Pringle who produced many of the plays in this book during
her time at Clean Break. She is greatly missed.*

Contents

Clean Break

Clean Break is a women's theatre company established by two women prisoners in 1979 at HMP Askham Grange in Yorkshire. For forty years we have used theatre to transform the lives of women with criminal justice experience. Our award-winning theatre productions share the often hidden stories of women and crime with audiences. We are proud to have co-produced our new plays with dozens of UK theatres, including the Royal Court Theatre, Manchester Royal Exchange, Birmingham Rep, Theatr Clwyd, The Royal Shakespeare Company and Soho Theatre. Beyond this, our audiences include women in prisons and non-typical theatre audiences including the probation service, Parole Board, frontline drug and alcohol services and festivals.

For the past twenty years we have engaged thousands of women on the fringes or with experience of the criminal justice system (our Members) from our women-only building in Kentish Town, North London – a safe space where learning happens and transformation becomes possible. The programme's success has grown a generation of highly skilled and confident alumni, many of whom (70 per cent) have gone on to further studies, employment or longer-term volunteering.

Clean Break has been fortunate to work with many extraordinary writers and creative teams over the past forty years. One of our co-founders is a writer, and, alongside our Members, groundbreaking plays have been the bedrock of the company. Many of the artists we work with covet their time with Clean Break and have been articulate about how formative their time with us has been. Lucy Kirkwood put it like this:

As an artist it has inspired and sustained me creatively in brilliant and unexpected ways … . [I was] afforded rare and very special chances to push myself as a writer or do things that aren't possible elsewhere.

The process of writing a Clean Break commission has taken many different incarnations, and in this anthology we have tried to encapsulate some of the journeys the writers represented have gone on. Included in the collection are a number of monologues by women we have engaged with while delivering residencies in prisons as well as work by current Members and those who are now progressing as writers.

We created this book to celebrate and highlight the impact that Clean Break has had on women's lives and the UK theatre sector over the past forty years.

Clean Break is dependent on funding and donations. If you would like to donate to us, please go to www.cleanbreak.org.uk.

Introduction

Arriving at Clean Break in 1997, I was excited to find that the company would shortly be producing Rebecca Prichard's *Yard Gal*, with the Royal Court Theatre. I soon came to realise that here was no ordinary commissioning process and that each Clean Break play comes out of a unique commitment to creative collaboration between writers and women with lived experience of criminal justice. Rebecca, like all our commissioned writers, had been deeply immersed in the world of women, crime and justice, delivering residencies and workshops in prisons and community settings, and participating in conversations and debate about what she had found. I saw how mutual respect and generosity on both sides underpinned this delicate relationship which the company nurtured with such skill and originality. This kind of relationship has been crafted and fine-tuned over many years of commissioning and producing plays; it explains why the Clean Break commission has become such a coveted opportunity among women playwrights. This was important early learning for me and I am proud to say that this ethos of collaboration is as true today as it was when the company launched itself on the UK fringe theatre scene in the late 1970s.

Women's criminalization and incarceration is at the heart of the Clean Break commission and offers unlimited scope to explore all aspects of a woman's experience as she navigates crime, justice and punishment. I have seen how this very specific brief has stimulated great creativity among our writers, who have opened themselves up for an adventurous time and have found their practice, and often their very sense of self, challenged. Courage to dig deep and ask big questions of the world and themselves is a characteristic of the writers we have worked with – and is essential, given what they uncover. Each writer has grasped the opportunity with a great sense of responsibility and integrity, bringing their own ideas and politics to the company and then allowing themselves to be stretched, provoked and thereby often changed. What they discover can leave them shocked, full of fury or devastated by the broken system they witness. It fuels them to write what many describe as their most important play.

These monologues offer unparalleled opportunities for female performers to take the space – not regardless of their backgrounds but because of them, reflecting the women caught up in the criminal justice system. This collection is a rich and diverse representation of voices including parts for working-class women, young women, older women and women of colour. They are monologues for performers who do not see themselves reflected elsewhere and for women who want to embody complex, flawed and brave parts. The legacy of these plays on the theatre landscape is a continuing rich resource of opportunities for women actors and a reminder of the range and complexity of women's experiences. This needs to be reflected in contemporary drama – not least of all to re-balance the ongoing dominance of the male narrative and the underrepresentation of women writers on some of our biggest stages.

Many women writers and performers find their voice and begin their careers with Clean Break – finding confidence and openings in the company's all-women team. We have been excited to discover new talent from women with lived experience of criminal justice through the writers' groups at our studios and the prison residencies that our playwrights lead. Launching these emerging playwrights onto the new writing scene is a source of great pride for us and continues to encourage the wider theatre industry to take a chance on previously unheard voices. The collection here includes both new and more established voices and an incredible range of styles and approaches: from the poetry of Alice Birch's *Little on the inside* to the street language of Sonya Hale's *Blis-ta;* the comedy of Theresa Ikoko's *FKA Queens* and tragedy in Pink's monologue from Vivienne Franzmann's *Pests;* naturalism in *This Wide Night* by Chloë Moss and the rawness of Danni Brown's *Jadan.*

Another unique aspect of Clean Break plays is their ability to speak to different audiences. In the early days, productions were performed inside a prison and today prison audiences remain a consistent part of the company's touring circuit. After its prison beginnings, the early Clean Break company toured to theatres, festivals and arts centres and this continues today alongside specific commissions for specialist criminal justice and health audiences. For the regular theatregoer, the plays offer a unique and powerful insight into a world which they would rarely see. In prisons, the plays give the women strength, courage and often a mirror of their journeys. For other audiences in professional settings, the plays reconnect practitioners to women's experiences in humanizing and profound ways. I remember how one play we produced in a prison with a cast of prisoners and professionals left the governor visibly moved. She told the audience that she had learned more about women's resettlement from prison through that performance than in all her previous years working in the criminal justice system.

These different settings speak to the company's ambition to connect audiences with women's stories, stimulate debate and deepen understanding. This can lead to change both at a personal level and at a societal level for how women are treated by the criminal justice system. For our audiences, this is groundbreaking theatre, changing hearts and minds. For our writers, it is a great adventure and a new landscape to explore.

When I left Clean Break in 2018, having led the company for over two decades, there were two things that I felt most proud of. The first was the lasting impact that the company has had on thousands of women's lives – women who have experienced first-hand the blunt end of the UK criminal justice system. The second was the phenomenal canon of Clean Break plays which has left an indelible print not just on audiences but also on the theatre landscape. Selecting forty monologues from the back catalogue of sixty-five-plus plays, and including work produced from our Education Programme and from women in prisons, is a fitting way to celebrate this extraordinary legacy and to extend the company's reach way beyond its 2019 fortieth anniversary celebrations. So when Róisín McBrinn, Clean Break's Joint Artistic Director, asked me to write this introduction, I was very happy to be part of this significant moment in theatre history.

Yard Gal – the play that introduced me to Clean Break's work – has gone on, like many others in the company's repertoire, to become a widely admired contemporary text performed regularly across the world. In bringing together these rebel voices from across a formidable body of work, this book is a fine tribute to the company's remarkable achievements over the last four decades.

Lucy Perman MBE
Clean Break Chief Executive, 1997 to 2018

Acknowledgements

Clean Break would like to thank Sarah Banasiak at Johson & Laird, Suzanne Bell, Deborah Bruce, Maya Ellis, Jane Fallowfield, Michelle Greenidge, Anna Herrmann, Jennifer Joseph, Caoimhe McAvinchey, Justine Mitchell, Lucy Morrison, Lucy Perman, Ambreen Razia, George Spender at Oberon Books and the staff at Methuen Drama, especially Dom O'Hanlon, for their help in the creation of this collection. We wish to extend a huge thank you to all the writers who have given us permission to include their work in this book and to our valued Members and women we work with in prison, who inspire us all daily at Clean Break.

Monologues

Little on the inside

Alice Birch

Age: Any
Ethnicity: Any
Accent: Any

PRODUCTION HISTORY

Little on the inside was first performed at the Latitude Festival on 26 July 2013, directed by Lucy Morrison – then Head of Artistic Programme at Clean Break – before transferring to the Almeida Festival. The cast was Simone James and Susan Wokoma. The production was restaged the following year at Edinburgh Festival Fringe in 2014 with Sandra Reid and Estella Daniels. This short play was Clean Break's first collaboration with Alice Birch, who went on to write *[BLANK]* for the company.

CONTEXT FOR PERFORMANCE

Two unnamed characters, A and B, in reality occupy a cell, but they find spiritual freedom in inventing a rich and extraordinary world where they might exist together. Originally commissioned to be performed in the foyer of the Almeida Theatre as part of their summer festival, this is a short, minimalist but complex play about the love two women have for each other, and the power of imagination and storytelling to excite, sustain and console.

Over the course of the play, we come to understand how A and B met sharing a cell. B initially lives on her anger – kicking, screaming and using the force of it to keep herself alive – while A, barely speaking, retreats into an imagined world.

In this monologue, B describes the moment at which she came to understand A, and A invites her into the imagined world she has created. It is a speech full of love and wonder.

B   And I realise
There are Giants in there.
In You.
Giants.

Marching all around your bones.

.

I had learnt to listen. And she had learnt to talk.

.

When we Get each other. And I get to come here.

This patch of green.

That is in her head.

Where white-eyes sing up in the red mangrove trees.

And the sea is in the distance.

And sometimes there's an old couple sharing sandwiches in a rose garden.

It's like she's kept it in her fists. All these rages and laughs and whispers for ears that haven't been enough.

So when she puts these hot little clenches up by my ears and

Opens

I get them all.

And we sit here.

Our backs to the burnt bedsheets and the hair and the shouts and the walls covered in faces you're not sure will be there when you are back out in Air. Her sitting under a tree her heart all full and Me swimming. Swimming in a sequined dress

A sequined dress from the back of Mum's wardrobe

Not supposed to touch.

There's a creak on one bit of floor by the wardrobe that means you have to go on one toe and lean in like it's the Lion the Witch and the Wardrobe and I pull out that sequined dress and smear of lipstick and heels that don't fit and I dance like I'm swimming, I dance like I'm doing the backstroke and the butterfly and like the air is cool and a kiss and not hot and a livid punch. And I dance to Yazoo, I just dance to Yazoo in my bedroom whilst downstairs there's a little hot quiet storm as my mum has her hand over one man an hour's mouth or tries not to make a noise as her body shifts to a place where it isn't hers and later, later her face will be a map of blue bruises but there will be chips for tea but for now I am dancing like I'm swimming and the redwinged blackbird singing in the green plumtrees outside my window, my legs skinny and dancing and sequins falling onto the shit brown carpet like moss under the too big for you girl shoes.

[BLANK]

Alice Birch

Age: Any
Ethnicity: Any
Accent: Any

PRODUCTION HISTORY

[BLANK] was co-commissioned by Clean Break and National Theatre Connections. The NT Connections project commissions ten new plays annually for young people in schools and youth groups across the UK to perform. The need to meet the requirements of the Connections programme (something with a big mixed cast of teenagers) and our own (only female characters) saw Alice come up with the inventive solution of *[BLANK]* – a huge, sprawling drama about the impact of the justice system on parent–child relationships, in a choose-your-own-adventure style.

The play has 60 scenes in its NT Connections incarnation but 100 in total, the additional scenes created to be performed exclusively by Clean Break. The director and / or company can put their production in whatever sequence they like.

[BLANK] was performed on the opening night of the 2018 National Theatre Connections Festival, 26 June 2018, at the Dorfman Theatre by See&Eye Theatre, based at City and Islington College.

Alice has had a relationship with Clean Break for several years and was one of the creatives working on the last set of residencies Clean Break delivered at HMP Holloway with Róisín McBrinn and Lorraine Maher, before the prison closed in 2016. This is her second Clean Break play, after *Little on the inside*.

We are producing the Clean Break professional version in 2019.

CONTEXT FOR PERFORMANCE

Because of the experimental nature of the show, all the characters in each scene are named only A/B/C and do not have standard given names. Some of the scenes seem to link together or have characters in common, but this is not explicitly stated, and each time the play is produced, the creative team can find their own journeys for the characters. Often, characters' genders are also open to interpretation. All that is specified is whether the character is over or under the age of eighteen.

This character is a policewoman (we know her gender because the other character calls her 'mum') and in the scene preceding this monologue, she receives the cold shoulder from her teenage child, who is angry with their mother after she has been severely beaten at work.

In this monologue, the policewoman is trying to explain what happened, and why it's important she keeps trying to help, to her teenage child.

A   He had pinned his girlfriend up against the wall. When we got there, she had purple finger marks all across her neck. She was like, no no no, it's fine, they – the neighbour who called – made a mistake.
Again.
I've been there three times before.
Every time I see this woman she's been beaten up in some New way.
Body cam never picks anything up.
She's always Indignant.
He's always quiet. Polite. Lets her talk.
I don't want to press charges, there's nothing to say, yadda yadda.
I went there once and he'd pushed her face into her own vomit. She had vomit on her face.
He's kicked a baby out of her.
An actual fucking baby.
Out of her.
You shouldn't be able to Kick a baby out of a woman, that shouldn't be a physical possibility.
.
This time. She's hesitating. She's thinking about it. He's not completely thick, he's kicked her below the neck so we can't see it, but she is finding it hard to walk. She's on the edge of finally saying, yes please, yes please can you help me.
And he snaps.
.
Body cam.
Catches him kicking a door down, lifting me off the fucking ground and stamping on my head.
He'll go to prison now.

Black Crows

Linda Brogan

Age: 30s
Ethnicity: British-born Jamaican
Accent: UK

PRODUCTION HISTORY

Black Crows was first performed at the Arcola Theatre on 7 March 2007 followed by a prison tour. It was directed by Tessa Walker, the designer was Jess Curtis, with lighting design by Elanor Higgins and sound design by Ilona Sekacz. The cast was Crystal Condie, Sharon Duncan-Brewster, Natasha Williams and puppeteer Susan Beattie. Clean Break commissioned Linda in 2004. She ran writing workshops at HMP Askham Grange (where Clean Break was founded) in 2005. Her work in prisons and with women on Clean Break's Education Programme (now Members Programme) was a starting point for *Black Crows*.

CONTEXT FOR PERFORMANCE

Set in 1970s Manchester, *Black Crows* is a story of love, jealousy and hunger. Three women are linked by their love for one young man: his distant mother, Queenie; his loyal teenage girlfriend, Hazel; and his older lover, the passionate Leonora.

The below speech is the first moment in the play when we meet Leonora, as well as the first moment she met the young man. She is addressing the person she hopes will become her lover. Despite its content, the speech is a (successful) seduction.

In its mixture of confidence and vulnerability, this monologue is an indicator of Leonora's character. She is a strong, driven woman who is willing to pursue the things she wants and will not take no for an answer, but she also needs a kindness and support she cannot get from this young man.

Leonara   I may not be good looking. In fact I'm ugly. The raw born ugliness that sets you off on a path. But you see the cut of this dress. You can't afford this dress on no shop-keep wage. Used to look at myself in the mirror and think Lord God but you're ugly. But you see that about me. You see my ability to see. Two eyes I have. Two eyes to use. Watch them now – clear as a bell. Ugly. But that don't stop me. That don't clear my path. Watch me now. Straight up to it. Straight up to the path. Straight there in front of me. I want it. It's what I go get. Me see it me want it me get it. Clear in the eye. I'm ugly yes. But I'm pretty all the same. Look how she's pretty. Cos as my eyes are open so yours are blind.

What me go give you boy is pretty.

Jadan

Danni Brown

Age: 15
Ethnicity: Any
Accent: London

PRODUCTION HISTORY

Clean Break has worked with Danni a number of times in different prisons between 2016 and 2018. Danni wrote this monologue during a three-day Clean Break theatre writing residency at HMP Downview and the insightful authenticity of her writing style, combined with a sharp wit, shone out. We are grateful to her for allowing us to include it in the collection.

The monologue was performed by Danni as part of the residency but has not been published before or formally staged. It is an extract from a slightly longer piece including a scene between Jadan and her foster carer, and a scene between her and the shopkeeper.

CONTEXT FOR PERFORMANCE

Jadan is fifteen and in foster care. It is Christmas Eve. She has been sent to the shop by her foster carer, who says she gave Jadan £20 for groceries – but Jadan can't find the money and has been accused of stealing it.

Jadan is hugely distressed at being accused of lying; deciding to go and find her mum is a last resort.

Jadan   This woman is trying to take man for some ediot, got me walking up and down like I am walking the beat, this bitch really don't want it with me cos I'll let loose on her in a way she ain't never seen before.

No. Breathe Dan, cos you can do this, you been doing so well.

Well if I just found a piece of glass I swear I'll only do it 2–3 times, no one won't even know that I've done anything.

Ha-ha I would laugh if I weren't this vex right now.

I'm bugging but this shopman is being over nice to me. I know he rates me, well enough to let me kick it with him in the shop, but I swear he's holding a secret candle for me.

Cos I catch the way he looks at me when I'm stacking shelves in the shop.

I see it but I don't say nothing. Cos it might be nothing.

Arrh, what am I gunna do? Where am I gunna go? For fuck sake about I took the £20 – that bitch never even gave it to me. That face-t piece of shit, nah, it's big big Christmas Eve, you know about you're kicking me out how d'ya mean?

Arrh ha, I'm gunna look for my mum, she might still live there but I don't know.

What if she don't, then I'm stuck, let me try remember that number. What is it again 0208 3552 arrh shit what's the rest?

Fucking bitch if I had the money I would of bought phone credit ya get me? That tight piece of shit come mash up my whole Christmas. You're supposed to feed me, look after me, but NO, you want to kick me out over one piece of fuckary.

Whatever. I'm done.

I know no good is going to come from me finding this woman but hey, she's my mum.

Joanne

Deborah Bruce

Age: Mid-50s
Ethnicity: Any
Accent: North East England

PRODUCTION HISTORY

Joanne takes the form of five monologues, each written by a different writer: Deborah Bruce, Theresa Ikoko, Laura Lomas, Chinonyerem Odimba and Ursula Rani Sarma. It was first performed at Latitude Festival in July 2015. It was then performed at Soho Theatre, London, from 11 August 2015 for three weeks.

It was performed by Tanya Moodie, directed and developed by Róisín McBrinn and designed by Lucy Osborne, with lighting design by Emma Chapman and sound design by Becky Smith.

The production was revived at the Royal Shakespeare Company's Making Mischief Festival in summer 2016. Clean Break commissioned this play to try and highlight the pressure austerity was putting on services for women and the dangerous effect this was having on vulnerable women.

CONTEXT FOR PERFORMANCE

The play charts twenty-four hours in the life of a young woman (Joanne) from the time she leaves prison to the moment she takes her own life. We never meet Joanne but hear from five women who encounter her along the way.

Kath is one of them. She is a receptionist in an NHS hospital A&E department. She is working the night shift when Joanne comes through the doors and up to the desk. At first glance, Kath mistakes her for her estranged daughter.

Kath suffers from panic attacks and is struggling with the unmanageable pressures of her job.

Kath   Out the corner of my eye, I thought it was our Laura. In she comes, I thought, it's our Laura! Please God, let it be our Laura.

Just a young woman. Taller, but the same age as our Laura although she looked like she'd lived a different life, not like she'd been a kid who'd had her school uniform ironed and folded, because I never missed a day doing that, not one, on nights all these years, but I'd come straight in from work, put breakfast on the table with my coat still on. The kids never wore a shirt Wednesday that they'd worn Tuesday. I'd be in for them after school, always did a hot tea. I look at this young woman and I see our Laura, 'Who are you?', in my head that is, only 'How can I help you?' out loud.

She's crying. Proper crying. Tears falling out of her eyes and onto the tell-tale neat white lines on her arms. I say, it's alright love, take your time, and I hand her a tissue and she takes it but she doesn't wipe her face, just holds it. What's the problem, how can I help you? I mean it, I want to help her, that's the bit of the job I hold on to. How can *I* help *you*?

She goes, Help me Miss, there's nowhere to go Miss.

Always Miss, it's an easy mistake.

I'm not going back to the hostel, you can't make me, the men are off their faces, my head's too wrecked, someone's nicked my watch! My hands are numb, the voices shout me down, I'm rattling. Cos they've gave me the wrong meds haven't they? I took them but they're wrong. My heart's bursting, I'm dizzy I'm sick, I'm gasping for air, I'm falling I'm shrinking I can't hear what you're saying it's just echo and hum. I'll kick in a phone box and cut my throat with the glass, I'll rob some scissors and stab myself in the chest. I've made a tourniquet from a plastic glove, you can't take it off me because I haven't done it yet, but I will.

Section me, she says, I'm a danger to myself and others, I'll do what I have to do, I'll section myself if that's what it takes, just get me a bed.

Or maybe she says nothing.

I can't think now. Maybe she just stares.

Anyway.

There's a box for suicidal intent, I lift a pen, I tick it.

I say Sit down. I'll get someone to see to you. My voice is less than I expect it to be.

And I'm thinking, oh if I could just take her home with me. Imagine it. Her sat at the table eating toast, Mick talking about his fishing trip with the pub quiz pals, her jacket hanging over the radiator, her bag inside the door of our Laura's room. A cup of hot tea, I could heat some soup even, I could be a Mum for an hour or two.

Didn't Die

Annie Caulfield

Age: 40s
Ethnicity: Any
Accent: Any

PRODUCTION HISTORY

Didn't Die was first performed at the Arcola Theatre on 1 October 2003, directed by Cindy Oswin. The cast was Lesley Stone, Angela Bruce and Helen Ayres. The production toured to York, Edinburgh, Bath and Chester, as well as to prisons and Thornford Park Medium Secure Unit, and was Time Out Critics' Choice. Annie developed the play – which is a dark comedy about former secure hospital patients – through teaching writing classes in Thornford Park.

Annie was shocked by how many women were heavily medicated and incarcerated long-term, with no release date, and by how many of them had been through hugely traumatic experiences. The title is drawn from a conversation Annie had with a social worker during her research: 'She was talking about the terrible things that happen to children, how some get killed by their parents. Then she added: "In fact, the psychiatric wards are full of the children who didn't die."'

Sadly, Annie died in 2016. We are grateful to her estate for allowing us to include this extract in the collection.

CONTEXT FOR PERFORMANCE

Didn't Die follows two former patients five years after they have left a secure unit, charting their friendships with one another and with their former nurse, Katie, as well as their hopes for the future. While these women have experienced huge trauma both before their imprisonment and during it, the play is full of humour, allowing for optimism.

Dinah spends a lot of the play alone in her house, awaiting a visit from her estranged daughter. In this section, she discusses her time on the ward. She is an arch, funny speaker who has dealt with her traumatic experiences through humour and sarcasm – but there are moments of sincerity in here when we glimpse the effect these experiences have had on her.

Throughout this monologue, Dinah is alone, addressing the audience directly.

Dinah   Waiting about, sitting about. That's what you'll see on a psychiatric ward. That and an astonishing amount of smoking. Smoking like it's the nineteen forties and no one heard a bad word about it. Not the only thing that's like the nineteen forties.

Anyway, it's not interesting, no people running about naked saying they're Napoleon. Just shuffling, smoking and staring. Anyone taking their clothes off and yelling, 'advance on Prussia', they'd soon put a stop to that. ... I did once tell Doctor Mary I was Mae West, you know, completely pretended that's who I thought I was to wind her up, but she just told me I wasn't helping myself. I said to her, 'if I could help myself, would I be here? That's your job. Not that it is a proper job, psychiatry. Just rubbish, made up by some very peculiar men.'

She didn't like that. I didn't like her. Doctor Mary.

Obviously, I was in a madhouse for years so any psychiatrist will tell you my opinion is open to question to say the least. (*Pause.*) Your opinion, once you've been officially locked up insane will never count for anything again. Especially not to yourself. Because you've been told officially that what's inside your head isn't right, is so fucked, that you can't mix with other real people. That's the cell door that slams on you. That what's in your head is so wrong, so disgustingly outside what's acceptable as human, you deserve to be locked up somewhere like Broadmoor with the likes of ... Peter Sutcliffe. You're in the same place as men like him. (*Pause.*) We had tea dances with them.

Then there's a change, some policy change and you're moved to a lovely modern medium secure unit, all fitted carpets, nice Katie-type nurses, drama tutors, pastel prints, and god almighty don't tell the Daily Mail about the gardens, aromatherapy and the colour televisions. They suddenly introduce you to a new kind of psychiatrist who says, 'You have to help yourself Dinah, you are the key to your own recovery, you have to participate, you have to rebuild your life ...' And I said, 'Build with what? There's not a shred left inside me.'

Thick as Thieves

Katherine Chandler

Age: 35–40
Ethnicity: Any
Accent: Any

PRODUCTION HISTORY

Katherine Chandler co-delivered workshops with Clean Break at HMP Holloway and worked on the company's Education Programme. *Thick as Thieves* was co-commissioned and co-produced with Theatr Clwyd, and had its first preview there on 11 October 2018, where it was performed until 27 October. It then toured to UK women's prisons, Salisbury Playhouse and Hull Truck. It was developed with Katherine by Róisín McBrinn and Tamara Harvey. The production was directed by Róisín McBrinn and starred Polly Frame and Siwan Morris. It was designed by Alyson Cummins with lighting design by Azusa Ono and sound design by Elena Peña.

CONTEXT FOR PERFORMANCE

Gail and Karen are sisters, but they haven't seen each other for over twenty years. Having been brought up together in care, they were separated when Karen was thirteen and Gail was eleven. Their lives have since taken very different courses.

Gail's life is difficult and chaotic; she has been to prison, and her children have been removed by social services. Karen, on the other hand, works for social services and enjoys a seemingly perfect life with her husband and three children. She appears composed, together and successful, but we learn she has buried secrets and in some ways is as vulnerable as her more obviously damaged sister.

At breaking point, Gail arrives at Karen's office, uninvited, to try and reunite with her sister – and to get Karen to help her get her children back. Karen wants nothing to do with her sister. Gail reveals that she has been to Karen's house and her kids' school, which deeply unnerves Karen.

This monologue is a rare moment of honesty from Karen. She tells Gail this story to let her know that she still has scars from the past – but also to let Gail know that she is capable of retaliating if Gail threatens her 'perfect' family and life.

Karen   I was a teacher. When I was first married.
I hated it.
You know what I hated the most?
Accessories.
Hats, gloves, scarves, bags.
They were the bane of my life.
32 five year olds, all looking for a lost glove or bag. Bobbles, clips,
hairbands. Jesus Christ.
The tediousness of it all.

One day, I was sat watching the class, they were getting on with a task or
whatever and there were two girls, Laura and Beth. Best friends. They started
messing about with each other's hair, playing, you know. Like girls do. Laura
undid Beth's hair band and ran her fingers through Beth's hair. Properly
running her fingers through using her whole hand like it was a comb.
And Beth's hair is long, half way down her back. And Laura's got her
fingers right in and she's wrapping the hair around and around her hand
and then in a flash and without any warning, she grabs hold of all the hair
in her hand and pulls it, really nastily.
With a smile too.
So I got up and I went over to them and I grabbed a handful of Laura's
hair, and I pull her hair back, really hard.
I felt her head yank with the force. And her little fingers grabbed for my
hand but I kept on pulling. It was only when I saw that her feet were off
the ground that I stopped.
I didn't want to stop.
But eventually I let go and Laura drops to the floor.
And I had a handful of her hair in my hand.
She cried.
Screamed.
The whole class was silent and staring at me.
And Beth throws her arms around Laura and kisses her, hugs her, tells her
everything would be okay and then shoots me a look like I was the devil.
The whole class looked at me like I was the devil.
Which I was, of course. I didn't feel sorry straight away. For a moment I
felt like I'd done them a favour. Like I'd shown them that life is cruel.
And unexpected. And startling.

The anger still startles me.
It doesn't go.
It might sit dormant for a while but there are unexplained, unexpected
times when it rears itself.
I hate that.

Takes her time.

I walked out.

Out of the classroom and through the hall and across the yard, through the gates.

I went home.

Then I felt sorry.

Spent

Katherine Chandler

Age: Any
Ethnicity: Any
Accent: Any

PRODUCTION HISTORY

Spent is a short play by Katherine Chandler, which toured to universities and service provider organizations, with accompanying workshops, from February to April 2016. The play was commissioned to explore the impact of austerity on our Members and the relationship between crime and poverty. The play was directed by Imogen Ashby and had a cast of Clean Break Members that included Michelle Hamilton and Eleanor Byrne.

CONTEXT FOR PERFORMANCE

This twenty-minute play takes the form of interlinking monologues from three different characters. Nat is a feisty, funny, young woman who has enough optimism to get her through the day. When we meet her, things seem to be going well: Nat is in a good place and on the verge of a new romantic relationship.

This should not be played, as the character does not know what lies ahead, but things don't work out well for Nat: the new man she meets turns out to be violent towards her and, among other things, convinces her to steal the old woman on the bench's wedding ring.

But for now, she should be played with a spark and a devilment.

Nat   There's this old woman sits on the bench off the high street. And when you first looks it's like there's nothing there 'cept a bunch of old rags.

But then she'll move.

Lift her head, cough.

Sounds like she's coughing up her guts. She'll fart if she wants. She don't give a shit.

I sit there sometimes. She don't say much. One time I asked her what she was doing there. She told me she was waiting for her dog and then she starts barking. So mostly now I don't speak.

First time I sees him he's hanging on the bench, opposite side to her. And he's sat on the back you know using the seat for his feet. Fussing on his phone and I goes by and he says 'Alright' but I don't look at him. I knows he saying it to me. There ain't no one else around 'cept for her. So who else he gonna be saying it to? I walks by.

And she's looking at me.

She's disappointed cos I ain't staying.

Pause.

She's got herself some glasses now. They looks like she got them from the joke shop.

She asks me where my friend is. I says I don't know what she talking about.

But I do.

Cos I been wondering about him too.

It's the coldest winter since records started and she's on the bench with less clothes than I've ever seen her before. She's lost her glasses. I tell her she'll catch her death and she claps.

When she's on the bench there's not room for three.

I can see he's there again.

I walks on by.

He gets off the bench to watch me and I turns and looks back at him, all pouty and my nostrils is all flary. I got my hands on my hips an' I looks right at him all fierce.

And he grins an' gets a tab from his ear an' he lights it an' he looks at me an' he says 'why don't you join us'.

I'm smiling even though I'm still trying to be all fierce but my face got ideas of its own, and I says 'I'm not sitting where you been resting your feet'.

An' I turns again an' I starts walking off.

'Come and sit there then' he says 'I make sure it's clean for m'lady'

and he takes his jacket and he puts it on the bench and then bows all cocky like. Thinking he's the joker.

She laughs and spoils it all.

Cackles and coughs.

I turns and walks away.

But this time I walks with a wiggle on, if you know what I saying.

She stops laughing and says something. I don't care what because it feels like it just me and him now and I know he's standing and watching.

He comes after me.

I give him the green light, I knows that's what I did.

Me.

I did that.

Pause.

I ain't seen the old woman on the bench for a bit cos he don't like me going there and then when I sees her she's bald. I don't know she's bald because she's got a hat on but then she takes it off and asks me for a fag. She sits there in the cold smoking with her bald head and her no coat.

'What's wrong with your face.'

'Are you getting on about my face when you're sat there with a bald head.'

Then he comes, wondering where I been and she turns back.

Hides her head.

Says nothing.

He tells me I'm leaving and he grabs my arm and pulls me off the bench.

Apache Tears

Lin Coghlan

Age: Early 20s
Ethnicity: Black British
Accent: London

PRODUCTION HISTORY

Apache Tears was first performed at the Battersea Arts Centre, London, on 6 September 2000, directed by Nancy Diuguid. The original cast were Maria Charles, Irma Innis and Sally Mortemore. The play won the Peggy Ramsay Award. Clean Break took the play to Brussels for community performances with support from the British Council. During her research, Lin Coghlan taught a creative writing group at HMP Holloway on Monday afternoons for three months.

CONTEXT FOR PERFORMANCE

The play charts the relationship between three women: Sandy, a pottery teacher new to working in prisons, and the only two women who are taking her art class, both of whom are there for reasons of their own that don't have much to do with learning how to make pots. They are Viv, an older woman who struggles with mental illness, and the seemingly confident Merle.

In the early scenes, Merle seems to be comfortable in prison and to have several friends – she is not initially interested in Sandy's class and is very brash and confident. Over the course of the play, she softens and the two develop a friendship. This speech is a turning point for Merle, both in terms of being a huge change to her circumstances and being the first moment when we see the vulnerability underneath her tough exterior. In the scene preceding this one, Merle has been talking about her mother (with whom she does not have a good relationship) bringing her small daughter to visit her. She is devoted to her daughter and has been looking forward to the visit for a long time. In the scene following this monologue, Merle is almost catatonic with grief – so this is a huge moment in the play for her.

The monologue stands alone as a scene and is not delivered to any of the characters in the play.

Merle So there I am, early, waiting to go to the visitors' centre, early, thinking shit, so she's with my mother, I mean I wouldn't wish that on my most bitter enemy, but you see Vivienne, it ain't unusual for the grandmother to have the kid, and then when I get out, and I am getting out, then I will definitely get her back now that she is with my mother, and I want to fucking kiss her, even though she has never been nothing but one cruel frozen-hearted bitch to me, and that is no lie. So I'm waiting, smelling of shampoo and hope girl, hope is coming off my skin like rays, thinking of the bedtimes to come, tucking up my baby girl, and that is all, all and everything that I want from my life now, you know me?

And they make us wait, five, ten minutes, and I'm saying, what is the hold up, in my head, because I say nothing out loud because of not wanting no trouble, and still they keep us waiting fifteen, twenty minutes, and my baby is on the other side of that wall, my baby I ain't seen in some four long months, and they are saying there is some staff shortage, there ain't no officers to take us through, so we wait twenty-five, thirty minutes, and Jesus, you know me? This is doing my head in. Then ten to twelve they let us in, and she is sitting there and I cannot see my girl. Where is my girl? And all over the room there are these babies crying, all the babies who can't even remember what their mothers look like. All those babies that start to cry just as soon as they are put into their mothers' arms, because they don't know their fucking mothers no more, their mothers are strangers to them, as strange as the green walls and the plastic tables. And the babies just want to get away from the strange smells and the arms of the women they don't even remember. And I can't even speak, you know, but I say, hello mummy, because I feel like I am *her* baby, even though she ain't never held me in her arms once in all the time that I remember, and I say to her, hello mummy, and she looks at me, without even saying no greeting to me, and she says, 'they have took your baby girl into the social services, and it's no better than you deserve, and now you will never see that child again, and that's what I should have done with you, put you in a home, and then you would not have wasted up my life.'

And then she stands up and leaves.

And I calls after her, mummy, mummy, mummy …

Head-Rot Holiday

Sarah Daniels

Age: Any
Ethnicity: Any
Accent: Any

PRODUCTION HISTORY

Head-Rot Holiday was first performed at Battersea Arts Centre on 13 October 1992, directed by Paulette Randall, designed by Jenny Tiramani with lighting design by Jenny Cane. The cast was Natasha Alexander, Yonic Blackwood and Susan Gifford.

CONTEXT FOR PERFORMANCE

It's Christmas at Penwell Special Hospital (a.k.a. the 'Head-rot Hotel'), a psychiatric prison for women. A trio of performers multi-role as patient-prisoners Dee, Ruth and Claudia, their nurses, and as other characters from the patients' pasts who we meet through short stand-alone monologues. The below is one of these monologues.

Shortly before this monologue takes place, Ruth's mental health has been badly affected by a surprise visit from Helen, her step-mother, whom she was arrested for attacking, and the nurses have been angry at Ruth for what they see as ingratitude in response to Helen's gesture of forgiveness.

At the beginning of her monologue, Helen confesses to the audience that, before Ruth attacked her, she had walked in on Ruth's father sexually abusing her and chosen to believe she was mistaken, thereby allowing the abuse to continue.

This monologue stands alone in the play and is the only time when we meet Helen.

Helen   Weeks before she stabbed me, she did a lot of negative things to get my attention, but I acted like I hadn't seen anything. When she stabbed me it was like. Like she was trying to stab some life into me. I know that sounds bonkers. It was so frenzied.

It doesn't hurt being stabbed, not there and then. Too shocked I suppose for the body to take it in. Afterwards that's a very different matter. She was written off as a bad girl, always bad, took after her mother and even she abandoned her.

So of course when this all came back to me I started to wonder what had happened to her. Then I wanted to see her and say something like, 'I know now. I understand why. I don't think it makes it right, what you did to me, but I want to help, to make up for the years that I denied what was happening to you.'

I didn't just go to the hospital on the spur of the moment. I thought about it for weeks. Of course it gave her a shock. I tried to call out to her but after the momentary recognition she ceased to see me. I telephoned the hospital after Christmas but they said she was too disturbed to have visitors and perhaps, considering the affect I'd had, that it would be best … they were very nice about it. I thought I could write but then that too could make it worse, couldn't it. I wonder who I'm doing this for, me or her? Me, I suppose, isn't it?

So perhaps sometimes it can be all for the best to pretend things are alright. And if I can't convince myself like I used to then that's my problem not hers.

Trainers

Raina Dunne AKA Titch

Age: Mid-teens
Ethnicity: Any
Accent: London

PRODUCTION HISTORY

Clean Break has worked with Raina at a number of different prisons over the years and each time she has engaged enthusiastically with the opportunity to participate and express herself through theatre. Raina wrote this monologue during a three-day Clean Break theatre writing residency at HMP East Sutton Park. We are grateful to her for allowing us to include it in the collection.

The monologue has not been published before or formally staged.

CONTEXT FOR PERFORMANCE

This is not an extract from a larger piece and stands alone. The speaker, a teenage girl, is talking directly to the audience.

Ellie   When I was younger I didn't have much, always wore hand-me-downs, three sizes too big.

It's funny, my mum used to say, 'It gives you room to grow into!' Well that's not how the kids at school saw it. They would always laugh and throw things at me saying I was a mascot for Oxfam.

One day though I was walking through town – and I never looked in the shop windows, it always made me depressed, staring at things I could never have – but my eyes spotted these trainers, cream with a green Nike tick. They were the trainers of all trainers. I saw all the other kids gather round the windows, noses pressed against the glass, they'd spot me looking and laugh. Saying it would take me a year for me to save for them.

Well that was it. I was determined to get them and I knew that if I got those trainers everything would be ok. The kids at school would see and they would leave me alone.

So I worked for anyone and everyone til I had enough money, my fingers were blistered from all the gardening and washing up I had done. Well, in my hands I held the money I needed to buy them. I stared at it – I'd never seen that much money before – but I knew everything would be alright after I got them trainers. I went and bought them and all the way home I sat with the box on my lap, like it was a treasure chest. I gripped it so hard my knuckles went white.

Well the next day I walked into school with these trainers, my head held high. I couldn't wait for them to see. I walked into the classroom and stood awaiting the reaction. But all that came was laughter.

'Look them trainers are old now.'

That's my life – I am always behind, aiming for something to be like everyone else. But when I get it, it changes nothing.

I ran out and threw the trainers in the bin.

Fingertips

Suhayla El-Bushra

Age: 16/17
Ethnicity: Eritrean
Accent: Eritrean

PRODUCTION HISTORY

Fingertips was first performed at Latitude Festival on 17 July 2014, directed by Jane Fallowfield. The cast was Sandra Reid and Chipo Kureja. Writer Suhayla El-Bushra wanted to look at what happens when an asylum seeker is waiting for refugee status. The immediate threat might be over but the trauma she is fleeing from in her home country and the trauma of the journey aren't. As part of her research, Suhayla worked with the Asylum Seeker and Refugee Health Team at Staffordshire and Stoke-on-Trent Partnership NHS Trust, the Forced Migration Service and Forensic Architecture.

The play has not been previously published. The below text has been edited for this collection.

CONTEXT FOR PERFORMANCE

Fingertips traces the journey of Kidisti, a young woman from Eritrea, who crosses the Sahara and the Mediterranean to reach the UK. She had lost her best friend, Genet, when their boat capsized. Genet seems to show up, hiding in Kidisti's flat in Stoke-on-Trent, and the women appear to be reunited – until we realize that Genet has been conjured up by Kidisti as she struggles to negotiate the UK asylum system.

Kidisti is a young woman who has been through unimaginably traumatic experiences. In this monologue, she performs as both the immigration officer and as herself, directly to the audience.

Kidisti You didn't go to the immigration desk? They didn't take you to that room? With the man who stinks and the woman with the face like a hawk?

I had to sit with them for three hours. Really, the man was very smelly, I mean old sweat like this ...

I ask if they can open the window. I swear they look at me like I am going to escape. From a window this big. The woman she look like she never smiled in her life I mean she look like if she had a child of her own she would eat it. These are the people they put to welcome you. And they stare at you like this:

(*As Immigration Officer:*) Why do you seek asylum in the United Kingdom?
(*As herself, to the Immigration Officer:*) Please. I cannot stay in my country. They are making us fight. My brother he was taken two years ago. Two years we don't know where he is. My neighbours' son he came back from the fighting, he didn't speak. After two weeks they found him hanging from the guava tree.
(*As Immigration Officer:*) You look alright.
(*As herself, to the Immigration Officer:*) Please. I came through the desert. I was kidnapped and held hostage by traffickers. They raped me and I became pregnant.

If you tell them this, they might let you stay.

(*As herself, to the Immigration Officer:*) They hung me from a tree. They call my parents everyday as they beat me. They say if they do not pay £15,000 they will kill me.
(*As Immigration Officer:*) Those Converse on your feet?
(*As herself, to the Immigration Officer:*) They beat me daily. Then the bleeding starts. I feel sorrow but also relief.
(*As Immigration Officer:*) All that and you managed to hang on to your trainers?
(*As herself, to the Immigration Officer:*) My parents send the money.
(*As Immigration Officer:*) They're doing alright.
(*As herself, to the Immigration Officer:*) They sold their house. Finally I go to Misrata. From Misrata I go on a ship. The ship it sinks. I watch my best friend drown.

If you tell them this, they might let you stay.

(*As Immigration Officer:*) And you still found time to do your nails?

They both laugh at this. I want to tell them how we did our nails that day like sisters, that it was all I had to remember you by. I think they will never understand, these people who look at me like I am a thief trying to break in to their country, trying to steal their life.

I do not want your life. I do not even want my life. My life is finished, that's it. I just want to live.

Pests

Vivienne Franzmann

Age: Mid-20s
Ethnicity: Any
Accent: Any

PRODUCTION HISTORY

Pests was first performed at the Royal Exchange Theatre, Manchester, on 12 March 2014. It was co-produced by Clean Break, the Royal Court Theatre and the Royal Exchange Theatre. The play was developed and directed by Lucy Morrison. The cast was Sinead Matthews and Ellie Kendrick. The designer was Joanna Scotcher, the lighting designer was Fabiana Piccioli, and the sound designer was Emma Laxton.

Vivienne worked extensively in several women's prisons and with Clean Break Members while researching the play, and spent three years attached to the company, working in prisons and writing for Clean Break's Education Programme, including short play *Sounds like an Insult*.

CONTEXT FOR PERFORMANCE

Pink and Rolly are sisters and best friends, trapped by one another in a co-dependent relationship – drawn inexorably together by their shared substance addiction, their poverty, lack of choices and by the shared experiences of their chaotic and traumatic childhood.

The play begins with Rolly, who has just got out of prison, arriving at her sister Pink's house. Rolly is desperate to make a new start and has even managed to get clean inside, but with nowhere else to go, she is forced to stay with Pink. Pink is the more deeply damaged of the two. She suffered sexual abuse as a child. She is still addicted to drugs, and doesn't want her sister to get a new life and leave her behind.

The below monologue occurs early in the play. The sisters are watching TV (a *Life of Grime*/*How Clean Is Your House?* type of programme) in Pink's flat, which is a chaotic bedsit described as being like a 'nest'. Rolly is drinking water and Pink is drinking beer.

Pink is highly intelligent, perceptive and charismatic, but being on the margins of society, she has not had the opportunity to develop or grow educationally or otherwise. When we meet her here, she has been living alone, hustling to keep her supply going and waiting for Rolly to come back. She is enjoying the company – and the chance to show her sister what she has been missing.

Franzmann created *Clockwork Orange*-esque language to express the closeness of the relationship and the components of Pink and Rolly's world. Within it, there are elements of London multicultural, street crime, drug culture and child-speak along with the characters' pure love of language. Lucy Morrison, who directed it, said that halfway through rehearsals, 'we took a few scenes we had worked on, to share with a group of women at HMP Askham Grange. We were nervous they would find the language hard to decode. We couldn't have been more wrong – they understood it immediately and within half an hour of hearing the scenes were improvising in it, which was something we had hadn't dared to do up until that point.'

Pink (*motioning at the telly*)   I don't approve of dis show. I for sure
don't fuckin' approve. Dese folk ain't wellage.

Beat.

Dey's at severest disadvantage, innit. Look at her. Fuck's sake. Look at her
fur. She ain't groomed dat fur in … never … . She ain't never groomed dat
fur. The last time she had a shampoo an' blow dry was, like, never.

Beat.

She can't even converse proper. Just done mumble an' stare down at da
dust. She don't even make da eyeballs contact. Bet she autistic, bet she
got aspergers or summit … .

Dis is shit, man. Seaside circus freakage. Poor dafty.

Silence. They watch.

Can just imagine it, innit, all dem tv nobs sittin' round wiv their
Pret – a – Mange free rangey baguettes an' Flatish Whites, 'Oh I know
a filthy fruit-bat who resides in the council 'state at da end of my road.
She ain't been out da house fifteen years since the death of her beloved
mother. Let us propel a camera crew round an' get her to sprucify it all
up, honestly, it'll transformify da scuzzy dirtbag's life, literally, like,
literally like literally, like completely literally an' we'll be dere to catch
it all, as an' when, as an' when, as an' when, honestly, literally, like,
literally'.

…

Member when I had dat jobbage?

Beat.

It was shit.

Beat.

It shit havin' people teltin' you what to do all day. An' how to act. An'
when you can have your munch or your fag or a piss or whatevers. An'
all da other does are bitches, who chat dick 'bout you behind your fur an'
den arks you if you wanna go for a drink after workage an' try to fuck
your boyfriend an' den telt everyone he got a tiny weeny member. An' you
have to get up itchy early. An' you get home suckered late in da black. An'
you can't do what you wanna do. It ain't nice. It ain't nice or good or fun
or any of dose things.

Sounds like an Insult

Vivienne Franzmann

Age: Any
Ethnicity: Any
Accent: Any

PRODUCTION HISTORY

Sounds like an Insult was originally commissioned by Clean Break in association with the National Offender Management Service and the then Department of Health, for a conference on Personality Disorder in February 2013. Vivienne was Clean Break's writer in residence at the time.

Following the success of this short piece – which explores the experiences of women with complex mental health needs and the challenges of diagnosis and treatment within the criminal justice system – Clean Break produced a small tour of the show, bringing it and an accompanying workshop to organizations working in the criminal justice sector such as the Parole Board. This was performed by graduates of Clean Break's Education Programme and directed by Rebecca Manley.

As part of her research, Vivienne spoke to a psychiatrist who works with women with personality disorders in the criminal justice system, who told her that, while official figures were lower, he estimated that around 80 per cent of women in prison were suffering from some kind of personality disorder. Vivienne therefore felt it was important to represent a range of voices and experiences in the play.

CONTEXT FOR PERFORMANCE

Sounds like an Insult gives snapshots of the lives of women with personality disorders and their experiences in the criminal justice system. During her research Vivienne Franzmann met lots of women with 'different experiences and responses' to their diagnosis, 'yet all of the women seemed to have lived lives characterised by chaos, a sense of isolation and a feeling of otherness.'

Brenda's monologue below stands alone in the text and is the first time we meet this character. She is speaking directly to the audience about her experience.

Brenda   When the psychiatrist gave me my diagnosis, I felt like an ice-cream. I don't mean I felt like eating an ice cream. I wasn't about to leg it off for a Nobbly Bobbly. It was like I melted. With relief. I melted with relief.

Suddenly it made sense. There was something actually wrong with me. Like properly wrong. It wasn't just me showing off, being a bitch, being a trouble-maker, being a number one arsehole. I'd always felt weird. Like everyone got it, but me. The world, that is. Everyone understood the world. And it was like I was always swimming against the tide with massive waves smashing in my face, spitting out sea water and trying not to drown.

Once, when I was off my tits on acid, my mate Keeley, who was tripping as well, suddenly said, 'Oh my god'. 'And I said, 'What?' And she went as white as a sheet and she said, 'I just felt like I was you.' And I laughed and said, 'And what does it feel like being me?' And she whispered, quiet as a ghost, 'Awful. It feels awful.'

So when the psychiatrist told me, I was relieved and I said, 'Great, what can you give me? Stack 'em up, pile 'em high and I'll start popping them. Let's get this beast under control.' And he says, 'That's not how we treat Personality Disorder. We have a programme.' And I thought, 'Oh shit.'

Blis-ta

Sonya Hale

Age: Late teens/early 20s
Ethnicity: Any
Accent: Any

PRODUCTION HISTORY

Sonya is a Clean Break Member. She studied with the company from 2011 to 2014, and Clean Break initially commissioned her to write the short play *Hours til Midnight* in 2012. This was Sonya's first commission. *Blis-ta* is Sonya's first full-length commission with Clean Break. The play is currently in development and has not been previously staged or published.

CONTEXT FOR PERFORMANCE

Blis-ta depicts an intense friendship between two young women – confident, street-wise Kat and shy runaway Cherry – who share a deeply co-dependent, exhilarating and yet unhealthy relationship. After Kat meets Cherry on the streets, she is moved to protect her, but she also cannot resist drawing Cherry further into a world of substance abuse, which the two young women feel they can control but struggle to break free of.

The play is written in a language that mixes real and made-up slang, combining the rhythms of colloquial speech with a more poetic, stylized way of speaking.

In the scene preceding this monologue, Kat has pushed Cherry for an answer on where she has been living since leaving home. Cherry has just explained that she used to live in a converted white van, but that it had been towed by the police, and she cannot afford to get it out of the pound – meaning she now has nowhere to go.

Kat is clever, charismatic and unpredictable – she is a magnetic person to be around, and a real survivor. Until now, we have seen her rescue and protect Cherry; in this moment we see how Cherry can, in return, give Kat a hope and excitement for the future.

Kat   They [*the police*] are such fucking bastards!
Look at you all on your jaxy lonesome.
This makes me so sad.
My lickle heartical break a bit ...

You know what Cherry?
We don't need those bastards.
None of 'em.
Cunts that nick your white van, all of them on the street, look at them,
look at them running about like ants, fetching, carrying, running their
life away, running to a shit job and a rank husband, drinking coffee in shit
cafes is the only thing to look forward to innit?
Naa mate, naa we is destined mate, bigger better things!

We has got it all ahead of us ... . Imagine ... . Rampage!

Imagine if we could get your white van. Imagine if we got it.
Me and you, just flipping got it out the pound.
And we could like just fucking drive innit?
Wind in our hair and shit
Boots on, accelerating,
Foot down
Short skirts, nails painted, music fucking blasting
And you could show me all those places that you went to
And we could find more, endless fucking beauty, hills, valleys, trees,
You could show me you mad fucking misty morning sunbeam innit?
Doors wide open
Drive,
Drive,
Driving
Dutty ass gal apocalypse riders innit?

Do ya fucking know what?
We should.

Daddycation

Katie Hims

Age: Late teens/early 20s
Ethnicity: Any
Accent: Any

PRODUCTION HISTORY

Daddycation was a play Katie was working on during her attachment with Clean Break that ultimately was not staged – instead, Katie took the central ideas and reworked them into the play that became *Billy the Girl*. *Billy the Girl* was performed at Soho Theatre from October to November 2013 and toured to women's prisons across the UK. The play followed Billy, a young woman returning home to live with her mother and half-sister after being released from prison.

The character of Billy has some similarities to the lead character of *Daddycation*, Jess.

CONTEXT FOR PERFORMANCE

In this very early draft, the story differs from *Billy the Girl* in lots of ways, but the play is still about a young woman – Jess – returning home to stay with her mother and half-sister after being in prison. Jess is close to her half-sister but has a difficult relationship with her mother, who she hasn't forgiven for putting her in care when she was a child.

Partly due to her fractious relationship with her step-dad, Jess grew up desperate to discover who her real dad was; she had a fantasy when she was little that the man who worked in the corner shop was her biological father, and in her head, she called him Daddycation.

In this scene, Jess is on her sister's bed, talking to her before they fall asleep. She is aware of the humour of the story she is telling – but it is also a story about their shared childhood that Jess' sister has never heard before, and in that sense is both comic and confessional.

Jess   When I was little I wanted to break a record. And be on the TV, be on *Record Breakers* with Roy Castle. Roy Castle who played the trumpet at the end and sang Daddycation Daddycation that's what you need. If you want to be a Record Breaker. Yeah. (The yeah went on a bit, it was more like yeeeaaah.) I really wanted to be on the programme, only I didn't know who Daddycation was or where to find him.

I didn't know what record I could break either. I couldn't run all that fast and I knew I was never going to grow as tall as a giant. And then I thought if I could learn to tap dance then I could do the longest tap dance ever danced. And I had this plan that I could get Amanda Reece to teach me. She was in our road and she went to dancing lessons on a Saturday morning cos I'd see her later on still in her dancing clothes – these silver sequins on her shoes – and I thought I'll ask Amanda Reece to teach me – like just the basics.

Well I asked her and she said no.

She said I needed the shoes. That to do tap you had to have shoes that made the noise. And if I didn't have the shoes then she couldn't teach me anything and I ended up biting her.

I bit her on the hand til she bled.

They moved to Stoke on Trent after that.

So that was the end of that.

And then when I grew up I realised it wasn't Daddycation Roy Castle was singing. It was Dedication. Dedication, that's what you need. If you want to be a record breaker. Yeeeeaaah.

Shall I turn the light out?

The Garden Girls

Jacqueline Holborough

Age: 30s
Ethnicity: Any
Accent: Middle class

PRODUCTION HISTORY

Jacqueline co-founded Clean Break in 1979 with Jenny Hicks at HMP Askham Grange.

Jacqueline wrote several acclaimed plays for the company, including *The Garden Girls*, which was first performed at the Bush Theatre, London, on 6 August 1986, directed by Simon Stokes. The cast was Maureen O'Brien, Sophie Thompson, Suzette Llewellyn, Doreen Mantle and Maggie McCarthy. The designer was Geoff Rose.

The play won two Time Out London Theatre Awards (1987), including Best Play, and was nominated for an Evening Standard Drama Award in 1987. *The Garden Girls* was later adapted for radio and aired on BBC Radio in August 1993.

CONTEXT FOR PERFORMANCE

The play follows a group of women who are all on 'garden duty' in a verdant open prison. They are of varying ages and backgrounds: some are in prison for the first time, while others have been there many times.

Mary is a middle-class businesswoman, out of her depth in prison and struggling with the uncertainty around her endlessly delayed parole hearing. Over the course of the play, she forms an uneasy friendship with Jock, who has been in and out of prison for much of her life and is very hardened to it. Holborough uses their relationship to explore the characters' differences in class and background despite the apparent similarity of their situation – but the sincerity of their friendship, which eventually becomes a romance, transcends the women's differences.

In this scene, which occurs late in the play, Mary – who has, at times, struggled to make friends, and who has had a semi-antagonistic relationship with Jock in particular – opens up to Jock about one of her most difficult experiences in prison. Although the story is an emotive one for her, she is trying to play down her feelings about it, to master them. This is characteristic of Mary and how she deals with the unexpected adversity of being in prison, but shortly after this monologue, we see her break down for the first time, cementing her bond with Jock.

Mary   'Pride and principles before pay and privileges.'

It was scrawled on the lock-up wall. Betty Maudsley probably.

I thought about Betty, and all the other women who'd been put in that place, not even a proper cell, just a store room with a mattress on the floor and a bucket. I couldn't even see out of the window, it was frosted glass. There was no sound at all. It seemed faintly ridiculous, here in this mock Tudor mansion in the beautiful Yorkshire countryside, to be kept like a child shut under the stairs for some minor misdemeanour. I couldn't find any sense in it. I lost track of time.

One day I saw a spider on the wall, with thick black legs. I was lying on the floor, staring at it. I thought, it's all right for you, you can just crawl away, find a crack somewhere and escape. But it never moved. It was dead. Finally I couldn't bear to see it clinging there any longer so I plucked it off the wall, and then I realised that it was a piece of scalp. A fragment of human scalp. I wet myself. I was so frightened I screamed for half an hour and no one came. I pounded on the door till my hands bled and nobody came.

Killers

Jacqueline Holborough

Age: Mid-20s to late 30s
Ethnicity: Any
Accent: Any

PRODUCTION HISTORY

Killers was first performed by the playwright at the Pleasance Theatre, Edinburgh, in August 1980. Clean Break toured the show the same year. The play was produced for radio by BBC Radio 4 in 1982 as *Wednesday Is Yoga Day*, directed by Kay Patrick, and was produced on television by Longshot Productions for Channel Four in 1984, directed by Bob Long. The play is set in the female maximum-security unit at HMP Durham, which closed in 2005. The unit was originally converted to hold notorious male prisoners (including the Great Train Robbers) in the 1960s, but was found to be psychologically unsuitable and after two damning reports was closed in 1971. A year or so later, the unit was re-opened for women prisoners.

There have only ever been a handful of women in Britain requiring such a high level of security: the Prison Department filled the thirty-six places on the unit with other categories including some ordinary prisoners on shorter sentence – this is the position the character speaking is in.

Killers was toured by Clean Break as part of a campaign to draw attention to conditions in the unit in the 1980s; the unit was controversial from the mid-1970s until it was finally closed in 2005.

CONTEXT FOR PERFORMANCE

This character is called only 'the prisoner' and is not named in the play. She is a first-time prisoner, baffled by what has happened to her, and is alone in her cell throughout the piece, addressing the audience directly. She has been in prison for just over four weeks and she's lonely and homesick; she talks fondly about her friends back in London and wonders what they are up to and what she is missing out on.

Although we don't know why she has ended up in prison, she talks about having wanted an 'adventure', and we can construe that she has not been in contact with the police before this isolated event, and prison is an extreme and unexpected experience for her.

She is a funny, intelligent speaker, but is struggling with her sense of loneliness and isolation, the dismal conditions of the unit, her shame at being in prison and, as a result of all of this, with experiencing suicide ideation.

The extract below occurs part way through the play, building on information she has given us about her day-to-day life and relationship with the people she has met, including the other women on the unit and the guards. The guard she talks about most is Mrs Thomas, who seems to have taken an interest in her. Speech in speechmarks is her quoting other characters, remembering things they have said to her.

When she re-lives the visit from her parents, she is speaking sometimes to the audience, and sometimes directly to her imagined parents.

The Prisoner   Counselling the officers is an important role in a prisoner's life. Keeping them happy through the long shifts can be very rewarding. And Mrs Thomas almost likes me. She thinks that I might understand. She'd bring me biscuits, sneak me the odd cup of coffee from the Officer's Mess. But it's more than her job is worth. A packet of biscuits today – a pair of scissors tomorrow. Backs straighten, jaws harden, and so we go on in a kind of confused contempt punctuated by occasional touches of sympathy, like when she saw my parents on a visit. She thought they were nice people. I suppose everybody's parents seem like nice people.

'What on earth must they think of you – in here?'

My father was drunk. Discreetly. Six barley wines in the pub on the corner to help him face the ordeal. Get him down the rabbit hole to his little Alice at the bottom. He managed a smile.

She remembers the visit.

– Oh, yes. Sure, Dad. I'm having a good time. First class, Dad, first class.

Mother has been crying. She hopes I won't notice. She fills up ten minutes with complaints about the lavatory facilities on the motorway; Auntie Florrie's bad fall last week; cousin Philip's new job at the garage and will I be allowed the nice pot plant she's brought?

– Am I? Yes, I feel very well. Yes, eating everything they put in front of me. Of course I'm not worrying about you.

The fact that my father looks like a sick old man and you haven't stopped crying in the kitchen for weeks means nothing to me.

She's determined to sound positive.

– Yes, Dad. Very like the Army I should imagine. Rolling cigarettes out of tea leaves, spit and polish, deprivation of soft egg yolks, yes – all that.

Pause.

How absurd it seems that we should be kept here like this. In separate little compartments. Filed away. For three years … or thirty, a matter of numbers. What you or anyone else is supposed to have done recedes into a dusty pile of paper and ceases to have much meaning. Everyone behaving as though trees and grass no longer exist. Animals and small children almost extinct. Private conversation, personal actions and life away from the antiseptic glare – all a long time ago.

Even after a few days it seems … acceptable. No-one complains.

FKA Queens

Theresa Ikoko

Age: 19
Ethnicity: Any performer of colour
Accent: Any

PRODUCTION HISTORY

FKA Queens was co-commissioned by the Bush Theatre and Clean Break in February 2017. At the time of publication, the play is still in development and has yet to be produced.

CONTEXT FOR PERFORMANCE

FKA Queens is about a group of women who find themselves in the same house, at the same time, connected by their varying degrees of acquaintance with one man – with varying degrees of involvement in his drug dealing.

Here, Ngozi re-enacts falling for D – and other bodily impulses. She is smart, stylish and thinks she's streetwise.

Ngozi   Every time he looks at me, I look at my feet.
My thighs stick to the leather car seat.
'I'm not'
He asks why I'm acting shy,
I lie.
I wind the window down a bit. Let the music escape through its crack.
Just enough to turn a few heads. And if people happen to notice me in the
passenger's seat of this black
Audi TT,
with Dennis next to me …

Ngozi *smiles, shrugs.*

'Only child. Visual Merchandising.'
My second lie. I just work on the shop
Floor, but once, I suggested we put the black converse at the top
of the display.
He says how I'm different when I offer to pay
Half the bill. He, of course, declines,
Reaches for his pocket I reach for mine,
I put up enough of a protest
To pass his test.
He pulls out a wad of cash. And the waiter looks uncomfortable
And I just stare at the table.
It's a lot of cash. Too much almost.
I feel like I've been talking the most.
'Tell me more about you. You're so mysterious.'
Cringe. So cliché.
I shovel food in my mouth while I think of what to say.
'I don't know. Anything … . Like, what do you do?'
He says, 'A bit of this. A bit of that.'
Looking down at his ringing phone.
I try not to let it distract.
He says he flipped his student loan.
Multiplied that, now his money makes its own money.
I look at the ringing cheap Nokia curiously.
It's not the same phone he uses to FaceTime me. There's something about
him that I can't quite … .
Oh … whoa … My belly's growling.
So I start talking loudly.
(Shouting.) 'What's your favourite colour?'
The first thing that comes out.

Now I sound like I'm 12 or there about.
Great. But he smiles, looks me up and down, licks his lips and says
'brown' ... .
Damn!
But, my stomach won't stop bubbling.
I can't tell if it's nerves troubling
Me. It feels like a pot of chilli
Boiling up inside of me.
'Sorry, I just ... . Going to go and powder my nose.'
Don't even know what that means.
I see them say it on TV.
I stand. Clench and try and glide across the room
And as soon as I'm out of his view,
I power walk to the loos.

Ngozi *pulls down her trousers and sits on the toilet.*

It. Is. An. Explosion as soon as I touch the seat.

Firm

Daisy King

Age: Late 50s/early 60s
Ethnicity: Any
Accent: Yorkshire

PRODUCTION HISTORY

Daisy has been a Clean Break Member since 2015, studying on the company's Education Programme until 2017. She wrote *Firm* for the Writing for Theatre course end of term sharing in 2017. It is a stand-alone monologue, rather than an extract from a full-length play. It has been performed at several different Clean Break events, most regularly by Member Jennifer Joseph. Daisy is currently on commission to Clean Break.

CONTEXT FOR PERFORMANCE

The piece takes place in a school hall, half-heartedly decorated for a leaving do. Stevie, a retiring PE teacher, is talking to her colleague, Gail, who has had too much to drink and has almost passed out at the table. Stevie has also had a few drinks. She is a cheerful, high-energy speaker, and the revelation part-way through the scene about why she is retiring should come as a surprise – the more incongruous the better! It's a light-hearted piece of writing and there are a lot of laughs to be found in it.

Stevie   Lovely spread Gail. Ta for the effort.

Bit sad to be leaving but it's the right time. Not as fit as I used to be.
I heard the year 9 girls takin' the piss 'cause I can't keep up ont' warm up
round the netball courts.
Crept up on me, like. Age. The ageing process. This retirement malarkey.
Good though in't it, means I can do whatever I want.
I'm gonna have loads of time. Just not sure what I'll do with it all.
Gonna miss them children. 'Cause it's about them. Not all that bullshit
about achievement records and final grades. It's the back and forth. The
watching 'em turn things around. The moment when you see 'em believe
in something.

(*To* **Gail.**) I'm going to miss you.
Wouldn't be telling you if you weren't passed out mind.
Sometimes I glanced at your diary in the pigeonhole in the staff room
while you were teaching and I had a free period. See what meetings you
were going to, what you were doing after work and if you were free for a
drink down the Feathers. Wasn't sure how I'd get to see you once I'd left.
Thought I might try to accidentally bump into you in Waitrose, the one
round the corner that you go to on your way home from school.

I do have one thing planned for my retirement. A group I'm already
involved with. Well I say involved – I run it, well organise, actually
I founded it.
A fight club.
Don't do the fighting anymore, obviously. Used to, but got a bit too much
trying to cover up the black eyes each Monday before registration and it's
hard trying to write on white boards with broken fingers.
The members call me Guv, as in Governor. My job is to keep it moving,
on the down-low, away from the Bobby Bacons. We'd been running out of
places, see. Used to use Trigger Dave's stepdad's place, wealthy geezer.
But we had to move on when he found teeth on the double-garage floor.
So I thought … I could do it here. Int' school hall. Only 'til we find
something more … suitable. After hours. No one'll know. Didn't think
anyone would be here on a Saturday midnight.

Turned out our headmistress is having it away with that NQT from maths.
Luke, smells like soup. I see them emerging from the hall cupboard. Been
disturbed by the noise from me and the lads belting one another.
We looked at each other. She looked around the room, then back at me.
Then scurried across the hall, sheepish like, hugging her heels to her
thrupenny bits and owt' door.

Thought it'll be fine. We both proportionately infringed ont' rules. I had grown men beating the daylights out of each other and she'd been giving Soupy Luke a whole other kind of beating.

Saw her Monday morning mind. She were a bit bothered. Gave her a wink int' corridor at break time to let her know her secret's safe. By lunchtime I was summoned up to her office.

So I said to her, 'Look, it's all hunky-dory. I run a little underground fight club in the school hall and you use it to put a different kinda kick in your life. We can work out a rota. We've both equally desecrated the rule-book.'

Which didn't get received how it'd been intended.

Told me I'd be taking early retirement. And that was the end of it.

it felt empty when the heart went at first but it is alright now

Lucy Kirkwood

Age: Any
Ethnicity: Any
Accent: English as a second language

PRODUCTION HISTORY

it felt empty when the heart went at first but it is alright now was first performed at the Arcola Theatre, London, on 7 October 2009. It was directed and developed by Lucy Morrison and performed by Hara Jannas and Madeline Appiah. The designer was Chloe Lamford, lighting designer was Anna Watson and sound designer was Becky Smith.

Lucy Kirkwood was Clean Break's Resident Playwright from 2007 to 2009, when she also wrote for the Education Programme, including short plays *Cakehole* and *The Little Girl Who Asked Too Many Questions*.

it felt empty when the heart went at first but it is alright now was inspired by the Helen Bamber Foundation's *Journey* exhibition in 2007 and was developed through extensive work with the Poppy Project, which provides support for women trafficked into the UK.

CONTEXT FOR PERFORMANCE

Dijana is a young woman who has been trafficked to the UK by a man named Babac, who had promised her a better life before forcing her into sex work. Babac has told Dijana that once she earns £20,000 she will be free to go. When we meet her at the opening of the play, she has been recording every payment in her little notebook and believes she is only one client away from freedom.

Despite her appalling situation, Dijana is a wry, funny narrator, who fully believes that she will soon be free. She is full of hope, humour and bravery. Almost the entire play is a single voice direct address to the audience.

In the original production, Dijana was Croatian, despite the fact that she was statistically more likely to be Albanian or Moldovan, as the artistic team felt that this risked re-treading old ground. The rhythms of the text suggest that Dijana speaks English as a second language, but Lucy is happy for it to be performed with any first language that feels appropriate to the character.

The playwright said of Dijana that she 'is a victim of crime, of gross humanity. But she is not a victim in herself. She has survived. She is broken, maybe to the point of irrepair, but she keeps going … [she] is still telling her own story, still trying to work out the world she finds herself in, still battling.'

In this section, Dijana is talking about a client she has been with. She speaks directly to the audience.

Dijana   Something strange happen this morning also. This guy, he come
and we fuck. Just normal him on top once then in my mouth and he come
on my tits but after he go something weird, he go

'ummm ... do you want me to call someone?'

And in my head I am like yeah do you have number of a dentist cos your
breath stink.

But I do not say out loud. I do not say nothing.

But this guy he is still standing there and my next client is coming and the
guy he is looking all red and English like meat and he go 'Ummm you
don't have to do this if you don't want you know'

And in my head I'm like uh, okay it is like none of your business! Shit!
Like I don't do what I want you know? I am fine. You think I stay here if
I am not fine? I am fucking great mate! And anyway it is not like there
are so many things I could do you know! It is not like I went to Oxford
University or something!

Anyway, I tell him, today is my last day, *actually*. That shut him up!

Yeah I say, tomorrow I will not be working here no more, which
actually is true, I say, I start new job in an office in the Canary Wharf,
which is a small lie but who give a fuck right. I say where do *you*
work? We are not sposed to ask stuff like that but I am just like fuck it
he is so nosy to me and anyway tomorrow I am out of here right! So I
say what is your job?

And he says I am a supplier.

And I am like yeah. And I yawn, to show how boring he is. Of what?

And he says pigs.

She raises her eyebrows.

Okay. And what do you supply to these *pigs*?

No, he say, I supply pork. I am a pork supplier.

And I start to laugh cos I think it is a joke, right? Like a shit joke, but a
joke, but he don't laugh. He say

My business partner has a farm. In Glaus-ter ... in Glauster. It is beautiful
place. The pigs can go anywhere. It is open fields. There is apple trees.
They eat. They sleep. They have a long life.

And then you slit their throat! I say. I just try to piss him off now, I don't like him. It is right he makes pigs, his eyes are like a pigs they are small and close together and he blinks like there is flies in them.

The meat is so good he say. You should taste it. You would not believe it. The difference in taste.

How much it cost I say. And he say a number and I laugh, I have a head for numbers and that is a fucking stupid price to pay for some bit of pig you can get it so cheap in Kingsland Road.

And he looks sad then, and he go, our customers can afford it. Our customers believe to pay for quality.

Who your customers, I am shouting now I don't know why, what shop you sell this in!

Waitrose, he go. And then I am quiet so he say, it is a supermarket, and *that* make me MAD so I go YEAH I KNOW. And I am bored of this now and his time is over so I put my bra on and that tells him.

Good luck with your new job, he go, as he walk out.

I see he has forgot to do up his flies.

Beat.

Prick.

Wicked

Bryony Lavery

Age: 20s
Ethnicity: Any
Accent: Any

PRODUCTION HISTORY

Wicked was first performed on 14 February 1990 at the Ovalhouse Theatre, London. It was directed by Joan Ann Maynard and the cast was Sue Rossiter, Caroline S. Sharp and Collette Johnson. The designer was Gaia Shaw, lighting designer was Paul J. Need and sound designer was Colin Brown.

Bryony visited HMP Holloway during the play's development.

CONTEXT FOR PERFORMER

Wicked is an experimental, cabaret-style play, with a handful of actors playing lots of different parts. All the 'acts' in the cabaret reflect on the justice system in some way. Rosie's speech below is her first in the play and stands alone.

Immediately before this speech, a door has been unlocked and Rosie has burst into the space. She is young and clever, with incredible physical and mental energy.

Rosie My plan was to dig an escape tunnel. Figured if I dug down 15 foot then along 75 foot then up 15 foot, I'd come up in the pub beer garden across from prison. Figured if I stayed on gardens I'd be having a pint in that pub in four months, thirteen days. I started digging on a likely spot. I was just starting on the top soil when a voice from a window yelled 'Stop!!!' That's the end of the escape-tunnel plan, I thought. But the voice said, 'Don't dig there, that's Ruth Ellis's grave.' I said, 'Who's Ruth Ellis then?' And the voice said, 'She was the last woman to be hanged in England! Dig somewhere else!' And I thought ... I'm standing with the edge of my spade in the last woman to be hanged in England! And it done something to my head it was like somebody had put a spade in the top of my brain and lifted off the top soil and there, lying in the earth were all these dead women. It was like I was on one of those archaeological digs, where you find old brooches and knives and bottles and nutshells, only I was finding these dead women. And I thought about that place ... Pompeii ... where that volcano erupted and all the lava just covered everything and everybody was stuck doing what they were doing that day, and I thought, suppose that happened here, this prison suddenly gets swamped with lava and hundreds of years later somebody like me is digging and finds this prison and all these women stuck doing what they was doing that day, what would the person digging think? I tried to get my head round that. They'd find this building full, full of women. 'What's all this about then.' That's what the archaeologist would say. A building full of women. Why did these women all live together? Were they some sort of holy order? Was it ... a brothel? Was it a place where women could go and enjoy each other's company? They all seem to be in together, in these small rooms. Then, when they swept away some of the dust, they'd find that some of these women wore the same clothes and had these belts with these metal objects on them. Was that a type of jewellery, wonders the archaeologist. And then the archaeologist says, 'Wait a minute ... this is a key!!!' All these women in the same clothes have got all these keys ... and the women in the same clothes are all outside the rooms with the other women inside. And the archaeologist suddenly puts it all together. 'Sussed it!' she says, 'The women in this place must be very, very important in some way, very, very special with very mighty powers because why else would they be so carefully watched over and kept safe?' And the archaeologist thinks she has uncovered the truth about this society. Its Women have such Mighty Power! I come out of my head because someone is saying: 'Rosie ... you turned over that flower bed yet?' And I'm back in the prison garden, next to Ruth Ellis's grave. But I'm not really back. My head's been turned over. Instead of seeing the usual gloom and grey, I see mighty power. No wonder they've got us under lock and key, we're mighty! No wonder they've got us under the thumb, we're powerful! No wonder they've got us on tranqs, our heads are full of danger to them! and instead of the escape tunnel to the pub across the road, I'm digging a new tunnel. It's through all this shit they shovelled into my head, mud to stop me moving, cement to keep me still, dirt to muck me up and I'm sowing seeds everywhere. 'You think you're dirt but you're not kid,' I say to one. 'You're the plant, not the fertiliser,' I say to another. 'Don't dig out ... dig IN!' I say. You're a lovely Rose. You're a scent of summer. You're a whole bouquet. You're a fucking wonderful flower garden!!! (*She smiles.*)

And you know how long it took me to think through all that? Three hours. That's the time it took to plant flowers all around Ruth Ellis's grave.

That Almost Unnameable Lust

Rebecca Lenkiewicz

Age: 70s
Accent: Northern UK
Ethnicity: Any

PRODUCTION HISTORY

That Almost Unnameable Lust was first staged at Soho Theatre, London, on 10 November 2010, as part of *Charged*, a collection of six short plays staged as a takeover of Soho Theatre. It was directed by Caroline Steinbeis and the cast was Janet Henfrey, Beatie Edney and Rebecca Oldfield. The designer was Soutra Gilmour, with lighting design by Johanna Town and sound design by Emma Laxton.

The other plays produced as part of *Charged* were written by E. V. Crowe, Sam Holcroft, Chloë Moss, Winsome Pinnock and Rebecca Prichard.

That Almost Unnameable Lust was staged again as part of *Re-Charged*, first performance 23 March 2011, also at Soho Theatre, adapting the pieces from *Charged* by Moss, Holcroft and Lenkiewicz as a trio of performances on Soho's main stage.

CONTEXT FOR PERFORMANCE

That Almost Unnameable Lust takes place in a prison and in the minds of the two women prisoners it depicts, Katherine and Liz, both of whom are 'lifers' or long-term prisoners. Katherine is now in her seventies and has been in prison for a long time.

Katherine and Liz are part of a group of women working with a visiting writer, undertaking research for a novel, but Katherine is usually silent in the group scenes: we are told that, although she can speak, she chooses not to. Instead, she opens up directly to the audience when she is alone in her cell, in articulate and compelling monologues on subjects ranging from prison life to childhood hunting trips with her abusive father.

Katherine is intelligent and introverted. She has not been able to overcome the things she endured as a child, but in these monologues she is able to take on a level of confidence that is unavailable to her in her day-to-day life.

Like most of her speech in the play, this monologue is addressed directly to the audience.

Katherine   The Writer asked us what do we miss? 'Men?' she ventured.
We all stared at her. No. Except for Gina who's a compulsive liar. Gina's
a natural irritant. Which is ironic as her life's mission is to please.
Which in itself is of course innately ... irritating. She has come to bed
eyes combined with a little girl lost. In a fifty-five-year-old that is not
appealing. Men are why most of us are in here. All I remember of my
marriage was the imperative to get away. From home. A proposal would
be like catching a train. The various suitors were simply timetables. Who
could take me away furthest and fastest. By the time I married I had to
wear a two-piece blue suit and hold my flowers permanently in front of
me. A farce. A lot of misguided fumbling. Not very clever.

What I do miss though ... is colour. Even people's faces here have lost it.
Lou is a greyish shade from top to bottom. She sits there, mouth slightly
open, breathing audible. Her teeth look as though you could simply pluck
them out from her gums. Forty-eight. Ancient already. Her face ... Prison
skin we call it. Almost translucent. A human jellyfish because she has
hit the outside air so seldom. Darker grey under the eyes. I half expect
to see her tea swashing around inside her mouth. It's not that colours are
verboten. I'm not talking gulag. But sweeps of colour. Swathes of sky.
I miss being able to look at the sea. I miss turning my head from left to
right following the horizon. Nothing here is on an epic scale. Apart from
the occasional Namibian scream. Or low Lebanese moan. Everything
else is contained. Cauterized. Like a wound. Enclosed. Measured. Even
a person's footsteps seem to diminish in here. It's the difference between
wearing slippers and boots. Or taking pills and not.

Typical Girls

Morgan Lloyd Malcolm

Age: Any
Ethnicity: Any
Accent: Any

PRODUCTION HISTORY

Typical Girls was co-commissioned by Clean Break and the Royal Shakespeare Company. At the time of publication, it is still in development and has not yet been produced.

During her research for the play, Morgan was the playwright in a theatre-making residency on a PIPEs unit at HMP Send, including writing short play, *3.48am*, for the women to perform. The residency was led by Anna Herrmann and Imogen Ashby, then respectively Head of Education and Head of Engagement.

PIPEs stands for Psychologically Informed Planned Environments: these are special units established to support women with severe or ongoing mental health problems, especially personality disorders. PIPEs units focus on the relationships and the social context in which people live. They are not a treatment; they are instead designed to support transition and personal development at significant stages of a prisoner's pathway.

CONTEXT FOR PERFORMANCE

Typical Girls is a play with songs. It follows a group of women on a PIPEs unit who take part in weekly workshops led by Marie, a musician and punk-lover, who is teaching the group to play musical instruments and form a band. Over the weeks the women come together as a punk band, which affects their relationships with themselves and with each other.

Munch only joined the group because she thought there would be better food at lunch and hasn't thrown herself into the experience as much as some of the others – but over the course of the play, she becomes the fledgling band's lead singer.

Shortly before this speech, she has got into a fight with another woman, and we have learned that Munch is in a bad mood because her girlfriend has left her. She is standoffish for much of the play, and this speech is a rare opportunity for the audience to see what she is thinking and feeling. Munch has a tough exterior and this moment is about the audience (who she addresses) seeing where that comes from: a need to protect herself after a lifetime of being hurt by people who are supposed to love her.

Munch   You. You once held me in your arms while I got over the shock of the punch. You once told me you were sorry and you wouldn't do it again. You once let me lie on the floor for an hour while you made food and tried to pretend you hadn't just broken my nose. And then it wasn't you it was you instead. It was you. And you told me you weren't like her. You told me you were better than her. And then you fucked me and never called me. And then it was you. And you thought I was cute and wanted to mother me even though I said my mother wasn't someone I wanted to be around. And you seemed kind and you seemed gentle. But you said that there was something about me that made you want to hurt me. That it was my fault. That I brought it on myself. You wouldn't leave until I called the police on you and even then you kept coming back. But then finally you were gone and next I met you. And you seemed just like me and I was wary of that and because of all the other yous and so we took it slow and you were amazing at first and you made me feel amazing but you got me into crack and you got me into meth and you fucked my head up and made me need you for the shit and then you were gone and I had to find another you who could get me shit. And then it was you and you and you and you and eventually when I crashed that was when you appeared. Like a fucking apparition. Like an oasis. There you were. And you cleaned me up and you gave me a reason to keep going and you made me feel something again. And you seemed, I mean you really seemed, you seemed to love me. You loved me. You. But then I happened. I happened again. Me. But you said you could wait for me. But I knew you were lying. Even if you didn't know it yet. And every time you told me what you'd been doing. Every time we spoke. I knew you were getting further and further away from me. And I felt like I was going mental in here thinking about it. And I felt like maybe if we didn't talk I wouldn't think about it. That maybe I'd just smoke cigarettes and listen to music and think about other women. Maybe I could forget all about you. You. You. Why the fuck would anyone wait for me anyway?

Amazing Amy

Laura Lomas

Age: Any
Ethnicity: Any
Accent: Any

PRODUCTION HISTORY

Laura was Channel 4 Playwright in Residence at Clean Break in 2016.
As part of that scheme, she wrote this piece for a small-scale, private
supporters' event, following her first residency at HMP East Sutton Park,
led by then Head of Education, Anna Herrmann. Laura was also one of the
five writers who collaborated on *Joanne*.
  Amazing Amy has not been published before or formally staged.

CONTEXT FOR PERFORMANCE

Amy is a young woman who is in prison for the first time, away from her
small daughter, Keeley, who is two years old. The full monologue runs at
about eight minutes, stands alone and is addressed entirely to the audience.
  In this extract, Amy is waiting to hear from her solicitor about whether
or not her daughter Keeley will be taken into care. Amy loves and misses
Keeley hugely.
  Amy struggles with anxiety and panic attacks; we do not know
whether this is caused by the situation with her daughter, but it is certainly
exacerbated by it.

Amy   After lunch is downtime. But I can't keep myself still. Thinking bout Keeley, bout the court case, bout what's gonna happen.

Got to get some air. Want to go for a walk but walking ain't enough. Want to go for a run but nowhere I can even run around. Head out to the library, least it'll be quiet in there. Give myself some time. Try and get my head in check. Go past the girls all sitting out by the smoking bench. Minnie calls over to me –

'How the fuck you doing?' she goes.

'Where the fuck have you been? Haven't seen you all fuckin' day.'

But I can't be doing with it. Head's banging, feel like I'm gonna do something. Colours going blurry.

Nina looks at us.

'You alright Amz? You don't look so good. You ain't gonna have a fit again are ya?'

Stand up. Got to leave before I flip out.

...

An hour later, I'm lying on the bed, knock at the door. It's Claire, my support worker.

Asks me if I've been doing my breathing?
Tell her I'd be dead if I hadn't.
Tells me I know what she means.
And I do. I guess I do.
Asks me if I'm stressed?
Tell her I'm fine.
Tell her I'm not fine.
Tell her my eye keeps twitching and I look like I'm having a stroke.
Tell her it's doing my head in. Tell her it's the meds. Tell her they're messing me up.

Asks me how I'm feeling. Bout the verdict? Bout today?
Tell her, t... t... t...

Asks if I've done my other exercises.
Says she wants to hear it.
What now?
Yea now. Will I do it for her? Might be good. Keep me grounded.

Take a deep breath in, close my eyes and open my mouth.

...

I remember when Keeley was first born, first time I held her. Smooth and wrinkly body. More like a kitten than a kid I thought. How's she gonna manage? In the world, in the big wide world? How on earth's she gonnna manage?

...

I am amazing Amy.
5 feet 3.
I have the whole of everything in my hands, all the past and all the future.
I have blue eyes that see, same, blue eyes looking back at me.
I am a Pisces. The fish.
My heart is a balloon.

Inside a Cloud

Sabrina Mahfouz

Age: Any
Ethnicity: Any
Accent: Any

PRODUCTION HISTORY

Inside a Cloud was the result of a residency co-run by Clean Break and Music in Prisons - The Irene Taylor Trust, at HMP Styal in 2016. The play was a collaboration between writer Sabrina Mahfouz and the women of HMP Styal, with the women contributing to the text Sabrina wrote through poetry workshops. *Inside a Cloud* was performed once, on 8 July 2016 at HMP Styal, for a small audience of invited guests, and was co-directed by Imogen Ashby and Vishni Velada-Billson. It has not been published.

CONTEXT FOR PERFORMANCE

Sophia is leaving prison tomorrow, and her friends have decided to throw her a leaving party and give her gifts – although obviously they can't go out shopping. Carly has just given Sophia one of her most prized possessions, her dressing gown. Carly is no-nonsense, honest, with a temper, and this is a moment of sincerity, where she talks about how hard she is finding it to be in prison, away from her children.

Carly   I'll tell you what it is, babe.
My dressing gown, I love it.
It's seen me through two babies,
wearing it in the hospital before I got too hot.
Wearing it while I was swearing at my man for being so crap.
Clenching it when the sweat was pushing me to another planet.
Wearing it again when I held them close,
when they crawled up my chest, like little lost lambs.
Now, it hangs there, staring at me.
Reminding me of all the things I'm missing out on.
All the days I won't get back, my babies like little lost lambs
but without a chest to climb up and find some place they know.
So it has to go.
I can't see it, but I can't throw it.
I want you to take it, just keep it somewhere,
you don't have to wear it, just, let it breathe a bit.
Let it see the sun in the park maybe.
You could lay it on the grass for a picnic.
Maybe. You know, if you can.

A Bitch like Me

Natasha Marshall

Age: 18–22
Ethnicity: Black British
Accent: Any

PRODUCTION HISTORY

At the time of writing, Tash is our Channel 4 Playwright in Residence. As part of her year with Clean Break, she will write a full-length commission for the company. On the journey to creating that play, having worked extensively with Brazen (our young women's programme), and with women at HMP Downview, she wrote this monologue. This character will be central to her full-length play.

CONTEXT FOR PERFORMANCE

This young woman has spent her life in and out of trouble. She behaves violently and is in and out of prison. In this monologue she is speaking to a councillor or a social worker who is trying to help her. This is not the first time a well-meaning person has tried to help her – but she needs a lot more than that.

Lesha   When my mum gave birth to me … and I'm sorry if this is graphic Miss … . But my mum said I basically tore her vagina to shreds. There was a lot of blood and stitches and pus and yeah … I mean you get the drift. She said looking at her vagina after giving birth to me was like seeing her favourite pub burnt down. But she says that's what I do Miss. I tear things apart and leave people to clear up the mess, just like her vagina. And just so you know Miss, my mum is actually going to Majorca next year in June to get a designer vagina and stuff … so it's all rejuvenated or whatever. But what I'm tryna say is, this isn't about my mum's vagina. This is about me. And Miss I'm telling you … you can't handle a bitch like me.

You see a bitch like me? I'm fighting doctors feeding me tablets to keep me sedated.

I'm fighting teachers and social workers and prisons trying to keep me segregated.

Fighting back tears.

I'm fighting my landlord who's saying, 'You're three months late with rent you need to be evacuated.'

Fighting with myself

Fighting with my mental health

I'm fighting that bitch manager from work who says, 'Lesha because of your lack of commitment I'm afraid I'm going to have to give you the sack.'

'Errrm no, you don't like me bitch because I challenge your authority and it makes you uncomfortable I'm black.'

Great now I gotta fight a random bitch 'cos she thinks she can flirt with my man.

I'm fighting that prick, that dickhead, that cunt, just because I can.

I'm smashing chairs on walls, I'm frothing at the mouth, I'm raging, I'm kicking in doors, who the fuck said I wanted saving.

I'm fighting rules and regulations that wanna see me fail.

I'm fighting the oppressive, caged up, boxed in system whenever I'm in jail.

I'm constantly fighting,

And you wanna know what the joke is Miss? ... I don't even like fighting, I've just always had to.

You're a nice lady Miss and honestly I appreciate you trying, but you can't handle this. Even if you tried, you wouldn't know where to begin with a bitch like me. And it's not that you don't care, because I actually think you're one of the few that does. But you can't take this on. Na Miss, you ain't been built to put this on. You can't handle a bitch like me. Trust me Miss, if you could be inside my head for a second you'd be shaking. Breathing through these lungs Miss, you'd be suffocating. And that's ok.

It's ok Miss! Because I swear on God, you won't forget a bitch like me. A bitch like me will be remembered. I'll be that big bad bitch every time, for the bitches who are too scared to fall out of line.

I fight for the bitches who cry at night. For the bitches that can't speak, for the bitches who are broke down, beaten and weak. For the bitches the world abuses and uses, this is for *you* sis. And you will remember me. You'll remember me. Years from now, you'll remember a bitch like me. A fucking bitch like me. A bitch like me!

Fatal Light

Chloë Moss

Age: Mid-20s
Ethnicity: Any
Accent: Any

PRODUCTION HISTORY

Fatal Light was first staged at Soho Theatre, London, on 10 November 2010, as part of *Charged*, a collection of six short plays staged as a takeover of Soho Theatre. The director and dramaturg was Lucy Morrison. The other plays produced as part of *Charged* were written by E. V. Crowe, Sam Holcroft, Rebecca Lenkiewicz, Winsome Pinnock and Rebecca Prichard. For *Charged*, the designer was Soutra Gilmour, the lighting designer was Johanna Town and the sound designer was Emma Laxton.

Fatal Light was staged again as part of *Re-Charged*, first performance 23 March 2011, also at Soho Theatre, adapting the pieces from *Charged* by Moss, Holcroft and Lenkiewicz as a trio of performances on Soho's main stage.

The play's research and development was supported by Inquest, a charity specializing in providing free advice to people bereaved by a death in custody. During her research on the play, Moss said:

> The vulnerable are constantly being criminalised for having mental health problems. The Corston Report (a review of women with particular vulnerabilities in the criminal justice system) was published in March 2007, following the deaths of six women at HMP Styal in just over twelve months [and] there has been slow progress in implementing its recommendations for the sentencing and treatment of female prisoners. There are still so many cases of women who've spent their lives dealing with mental health problems and abuse, who are then incarcerated miles from families, support networks, their kids. Prison is the final straw for them.

CONTEXT FOR PERFORMANCE

Fatal Light revolves around Maggie and her daughter Jay, and between Jay and her young daughter Aine. The play has a reverse structure, beginning with Maggie being told that her daughter Jay has committed suicide in prison, and ending with Jay telling Maggie the hopeful news that she is pregnant with Aine.

In this section, Jay has just been arrested. The monologue that appears below stands alone as a scene in its entirety, and is set in an interview room in a police station, where Jay sits at a table opposite an unseen policeman.

Jay   Janine Emma Hill. (*Beat.*) You can call me Jay though I don't mind.

Pause.

Twenty fifth of April, nineteen eighty six.

Pause.

The Aylesbury Estate.

Pause. **Jay** *sighs.*

Flat 33b, Thurlow Street on the Aylesbury Estate, Walworth SE17 2UZ, London, England. Great Britain. The World.

Pause.

No, I don't. I'm not laughing.

Pause.

Just me and my daughter. Aine. She's seven.

Pause.

She was at school. I'm not gonna start a fire when she's in the fucking house am I? I wasn't trying to hurt anyone.

Pause.

I poured lighter fuel on the floorboards and threw a lit match on them.

Pause.

It wasn't the *whole* flat, it was a section of the floor but it just went up, I wasn't expecting it to be like that. I got scared so I phoned the fire brigade. There's an old woman downstairs.

Pause.

No. I wasn't drunk. A can. Two cans tops. (*Beat.*) I'm not a fucking alky. It just helps sometimes, that's all. Softens things.

Pause.

Sometimes.

Pause.

I've never laid a hand on her. I wouldn't. I'd never touch a hair on her head. I'd die for her. I would. She's just this … (*Long pause.*) You know when you go Burger King? Or McDonalds. KFC? Shit like that? (*Beat.*) D'you empty your tray into the bin or d'you just leave it on the table?

Silence.

She empties it by herself. She's seven and when she's finished she picks it up and she takes it over and she puts it in the bin. I don't tell her. I don't even do it myself. I used to work in Burger King and it fucked me off when people cleaned up after themselves. I like to keep busy, y'see. It is fucking soul destroying, that job, 'specially when you're not on the tills. You just have to walk around with a brush and one of them little flippy bin things with the handle and clear up shit. Which is okay, long as there's shit to clear up. People think they're being helpful but they're not.

Anyway, she doesn't know that. All she's thinking is that it's important to clean up after yourself. It is important not to rely on other people to mop up your shit.

You have to learn to look after yourself. (*Beat.*) It doesn't sound much, I know, but it makes my head ache I'm telling you. We're walking down the road one day together. Couple of years ago. I swear down, she's like … four. And she looks up at me, face all scrunched up and she goes. Hang on … . She goes … 'In my imagination, sometimes I feel sorry for somebody but I don't know who they are. I haven't got a sad face but I just feel a bit … urgh. Do you ever get that?' (*Beat.*) Four years of age. I swear. Her soul is like this – Her heart, man. Her little big heart. She cripples me. She just totally does me in.

Silence.

Can I go home now please?

This Wide Night

Chloë Moss

Age: 30
Ethnicity: Any
Accent: Any

PRODUCTION HISTORY

This Wide Night was first performed at Soho Theatre on 30 July 2008, directed by Lucy Morrison. The designer was Chloe Lamford, lighting designer was Anna Watson and sound designer was Becky Smith. The original cast were Jan Pearson and Cathy Owen; it was later remounted with Maureen Beattie and Zawe Ashton.

The play won the Susan Smith Blackburn Prize and has been staged several times since it premiered, across the UK and in New York. As well as running at Soho Theatre, the original production toured to women's prisons in the UK.

Before writing the play, Chloë and Lucy ran a playwriting residency at HMP Cookham Wood with a group of long-term prisoners over three months in the summer of 2006. Chloë dedicated this play to the women she met there: Su, Vicky, Clare, Esther, Susan and Alicia.

CONTEXT FOR PERFORMANCE

This Wide Night explores the importance and uniqueness of relationships formed in prison – how they can, or perhaps cannot, exist in another context. The play's two characters, Marie (in her thirties) and Lorraine (in her fifties), met sharing a cell when Marie first came into prison; in this extract, Marie remembers that first meeting and how the frightening experience of going into prison was made easier by meeting Lorraine.

The play begins with the newly released Lorraine turning up unannounced at Marie's door hoping to stay for a while. The play is a tender but painful portrayal of two women at different stages of life trying and failing to support each other to start again as they struggle to adjust to the changing context of their friendship.

In this monologue, Marie has returned home from work at 2.30 am to find Lorraine – who is staying on her couch – still awake. Though their early interactions were stilted, by the time Marie left for work they had begun to rediscover the connection they made in prison. In this extract, in the quiet of the night, Marie opens up to her old friend. Note the stage direction at the end, that Lorraine has fallen asleep at some point while Marie speaks – it is never easy for these characters to fully open up.

Marie   My first night. (*Beat.*) I thought you was a nutter at first.

Goin' on about meditating to the sound of the fuckin' rain. I'm practically scratching at the walls and you're just lying there. Then you go 'The silence takes a bit of gettin' used to. You listen to your heart beatin' and you listen to yourself breathing and when it rains it sounds deafening.'

I used to do this thing when I was little. Raindrop racing. I'd fix on two drops. One would be me and the other one would be any kid in school who was doing alright, like if they had a nice mum and dad or a nice house.

Mostly it was Charlotte Hughes coz her mum worked in Greggs and put cream cakes in her packed lunch.

Sometimes my one'd stop and hang on another raindrop and I'd imagine that was when I went to stay with Aunty Barbara or Mr and Mrs Dent or Sam and Jason's then it'd separate and roll down and catch up with Charlotte Hughes.

Aim of the game was that if you got down first then you'd be alright.

Aunty Barbara, she weren't my proper aunty but she made me call her that for some reason, she used to say 'Not everyone can be alright Marie. The world isn't like that. Some people are rich and some people are poor. Some people's mothers work in Greggs and some don't. Not everyone can be alright. That isn't how things work.'

So I used to have me nose pressed against the window willing myself to stop hanging about and get down to the finish line.

Charlotte's raindrop usually zig-zagged along no sweat but if she did brush against another one I reckoned it'd be something nice like popping into a friend's for tea then she'd be on her way, holding one of them party bags with flumps and fruit-salad chews in it.

Once, David Harper was the other raindrop because he had a nan who knitted clothes for his action men.

Beat.

I still do it now sometimes. That game.

Silence. **Lorraine** *has fallen asleep.*

Lorraine?

Amongst the Reeds

Chinonyerem Odimba

Age: 16
Ethnicity: Any performer of colour
Accent: English as a second language

PRODUCTION HISTORY

Amongst the Reeds was first performed at the Assembly Box at the Edinburgh Fringe Festival on 4 August 2016, where it ran until 27 August before transferring to the Yard Theatre, London, running from 1 to 17 September. The original cast was Rebecca Omogbehin and Jan Le. The play was staged in a double bill with *House* by Somalia Seaton. Both plays were directed by Róisín McBrinn and designed by Rachael Canning with lighting design by Natasha Chivers and sound design by Becky Smith.

Both plays came out of Clean Break's Emerging Writers' Programme, run with support from the Tricycle Theatre (now Kiln Theatre), Bristol Old Vic and the Royal Exchange Theatre, Manchester.

CONTEXT FOR PERFORMANCE

Gillian is a young Vietnamese woman who has been trafficked to the UK (although, for the purposes of this extract, Chinonyerem is happy for the monologue to be performed by any actor of colour). For most of the play, Gillian, who is heavily pregnant, is living in a disused building, hiding from the authorities with her friend Oni, a Nigerian teenager. They are both in the UK illegally and, for different reasons, fear being deported. Towards the end of the play, we realize that Gillian is only imagining that Oni has been with her and, as her baby is about to arrive, she decides to leave the building to get help.

In this speech, which takes place towards the end of the play, Gillian and Oni have been separated, and she is speaking to the authorities. It is the first time we discover how she ended up in her situation. At this point she is no longer pregnant and is in a vulnerable position, in need of help.

Gillian   I want to be good for baby. I want to look after her now, Oni will help me. I know she is good person. Like my daddy ...
... My daddy who put his girl on a plane to UK. My daddy who trust his friend to look after his daughter. He trust Uncle. His best friend for so long. He trust him put me in study, look after me. He did for first few months but then student visa run out. He doesn't care. Like he plan it. I say I want to go home but he tell me he can't find passport. Then he say he can get new passport and I go home see my family. But now this time my uncle start to say I have to do something for his friend. He say his friend good man. Him and his wife want baby but she is old, and so hard in UK to get baby. He say they pay a lot. Enough for new passport, and for me go back to good university.
I have to stop school. The man come, and he come every day for many weeks. He come and ...
... He try to be kind. He bring flowers and chocolate and sometimes he stay to talk after. He also bring test for baby. Then one day test show two lines. He buy me takeaway food and give Uncle car.
I grow big. I am very sick. Every day eat and sick. One day Uncle say man give him money to buy me clothes to look nice so we go shopping in centre with Uncle. I look in mirror and I can see it. Baby. It is there. I want it. I don't know. Maybe I don't want it ... .
I go to toilet and there I see it. There where you wash hands is window. There is window. I see it and start climbing. I run so fast it feel like there is no ground. I don't see where until I stop.
(*Short beat.*)
... And before I am speaking to my daddy all the time on telephone. Uncle speak to him say passport coming soon. Now I don't tell him my daddy. I can't tell him. My uncle tell him I leave my study and run away ...
... How my daddy look at me now? Like prostitute?
They try buy my baby but I don't take the money. I don't take it. Oni will tell you ... . She make me brave. She stay with me. Look after me.

She look after baby too. She says my baby is special. Special baby girl.

Te Awa I Tahuti (The River that Ran Away)

Rena Owen

Age: Any
Ethnicity: Any
Accent: Any

PRODUCTION HISTORY

Te Awa I Tahuti (The River that Ran Away) was first performed at
Pentameters Theatre, Hampstead, on 15 February 1987, directed by Ann
Mitchell. Writer Rena Owen also played the lead. The production toured
to a number of venues in and around London, including Theatro Technis,
Watermans Arts Centre, Lauderdale House and Bridge Lane Theatre. Rena
was new to both acting and writing at the time, and she has gone on to a
successful career as a performer on stage and screen.

CONTEXT FOR PERFORMANCE

Toni is a young Māori woman who finds herself in an English prison for a
drug offence. With the assistance of her counsellor, she begins to confront
her past, her feelings about her Māori heritage, and to make plans for her
future.

Part of what comes up for Toni in the play is the loss of her brother. She
moves between aggression towards her councillor, a desire to bury things,
and a willingness to confront them. The memories she is sharing in the
below monologue are painful to her, and she isn't a character who finds
it easy to be vulnerable in front of other people – but the fact that she is
willing to share these memories represents a 'breakthrough' in her journey
and a growing trust between these two characters.

While this monologue was originally written for a woman of Māori/
Pakeha heritage, Rena is happy for it to be performed by anybody.

Toni   He used to take me to school. He'd hold my hand. We'd take the short cut through the park. There was an old archway made of stone at its entrance. Engraved in big capital letters, Moerewa ... Peaceful valley.

There were big oak trees on both sides of the road leading to the rugby fields. Their branches met in the middle, blocking out the sky.

Sometimes he'd leave me behind, run off with his mates. I'd cry. He'd get angry with me.

I was running as fast as I could to keep up with him. Suddenly, I tripped over, my knee was grazed. The skin on my kneecap ripped off, a flap of it still hanging, blood running down my leg into my sandal. There was a thick pine needle sticking into my big toe. I screamed. 'Frankie, come back, don't leave me.'

He came back. He crouched down. I put my arms around his neck, he put his arms through my legs – to give me a piggyback.

He stood up, and carried me on his back, through the tunnel of trees, all the way home.

Pause.

Why couldn't I help him when he needed me?

What good is your help, Sister of Mercy? You can't bring him back.

Mules

Winsome Pinnock

Age: Late teens
Ethnicity: Any
Accent: Any

PRODUCTION HISTORY

Mules was co-produced by the Royal Court Theatre and received its first performance there on 30 April 1996. It was directed by Roxana Silbert and the cast was Sheila Whitfield, Abi Eniola and Clare Perkins. The designer was Naomi Wilkinson and the lighting designer was Tanya Burns. As part of her research, Winsome worked with Hibiscus, a voluntary sector organization that supports foreign nationals, and black, minority ethnic and refugee groups serving a custodial sentence, released into the community or returned to their home country. *Mules* was also produced in Los Angeles, directed by Lisa Peterson at the Mark Taper Forum in Los Angeles in 1997 and was subsequently produced at the Magic Theatre in San Francisco, directed by Diane Wynter in 1998.

CONTEXT FOR PERFORMANCE

The play follows a young woman in Jamaica and a young woman in London who are convinced by the same powerful drug runner to be her 'mules', people who carry drugs onto aeroplanes in order to smuggle them across borders. When we first meet Allie, she is a runaway from outside of London who has just arrived in the city and is looking for accommodation. She struggles to find work and pay rent, to settle in to her new life, and is desperate by the time she meets Bridie – a confident, older woman who seems to have it all sorted out. Bridie pays Allie to travel out to Jamaica and return as a drugs mule.

In this monologue, Allie has just made her first successful trip and is completely elated. Up to this point, she's quite a low-status character, who isn't very comfortable in her skin or with her place in the world, and she's fleeing a difficult home life – but this experience seems to transform her, making her more confident than we have ever seen her. She is addressing Bridie in this scene, who she looks up to, and her excitement borders on showing off at times.

Allie   All through the flight I wanted to scratch my head, but I didn't want to draw attention to my hair. Besides, what if I scratched my head and the wig moved, then everybody would've known I was wearing a wig, wouldn't they? They might get suspicious. So I had to put up with this itch. It drove me mad. I tried everything; I tried to ignore it, but the more you try and ignore something the more you think about it, don't you? So the itch is starting to get worse and worse and I'm trying to find ways to get rid of it without actually touching it. I try to go to sleep but the itch won't let me. I try to get myself so drunk that I'll fade away in an alcoholic blur, but the drink and flight simply stimulate me and the itch is getting more ticklish. To make matters worse, I develop an itch on my stomach, so now I'm getting itchy all over and I can't do anything about it because I don't want to make the air hostesses suspect anything, and I can't go to the loo as this enormous bloke in the seat beside me has fallen asleep and I don't want to wake up him.

I wanted to scratch myself raw, but as soon as I got out of the airport, the itch just disappeared.

Going through customs was another matter altogether. My heart was thumping. I could swear that everybody was staring at me. I noticed this man at customs looking at me. Should I look back at him, should I drop my gaze or should I smile?

Then, somehow, I don't know how, it was like somebody else took over. This really cool woman who had no nerves. My heart stopped beating, there was this silence inside me. I felt full of this power and I just walked past customs as though I expected to be allowed straight through. And I was.

I can't describe the high, Bridie. I felt like I could do anything I wanted. Jump through flaming hoops, race with panthers. Nothing's ever felt as good. Then it all come back to me, every single official at that airport had somebody else's face.

Every face that's ever scowled at me, looked down at me, denied me. Headmasters, teachers, shop assistants, petty officials. I walked through customs sticking two fingers up at them all and they couldn't do a thing about it. One-nil to me.

Taken

Winsome Pinnock

Age: 40s
Ethnicity: Black British (including mixed race)
Accent: Any

PRODUCTION HISTORY

Taken was first staged at Soho Theatre, London on 10 November 2010, as part of *Charged*, a collection of six short plays staged as a takeover of Soho Theatre. It was directed by Caroline Steinbeis and the cast was Beatie Edney, Janet Henfrey and Rebecca Oldfield. The designer was Soutra Gilmour, with lighting design by Johanna Town and sound design by Emma Laxton.

The other plays produced as part of *Charged* were written by E. V. Crowe, Sam Holcroft, Rebecca Lenkiewicz, Chloë Moss and Rebecca Prichard.

CONTEXT FOR PERFORMANCE

When Della was younger, she had issues with substance abuse and addiction, and her children were removed from her by Social Services when they were small. At the beginning of the play, Della's daughter Nola arrives at Della's flat to re-establish their relationship.

Della is living alone with her elderly mother and is initially mistrustful of Nola – but when she realizes who she is, she is delighted to see her.

Della has lived a difficult life and worked very hard to overcome her circumstances. She is a character who has been through a lot, but remains strong and light-hearted – this speech is one of the first moments in the play when we get a sense of what she has been through.

Before this extract, Nola has heard Della's mother-her grandmother-calling from the next room and asked to see her. Della doesn't want them to see each other, as her mother may not recognize Nola and could be alarmed. Della is explaining that to Nola in this monologue. The two women haven't seen each other for a long time, so they are not entirely comfortable together, but there is a lot of warmth in their interactions.

Della   You'd better go. She gets anxious with strangers.

She's not very well.

Bad heart. Bad legs. Worse memory. Sometimes she's sharp as a button. Other times she don't know where she is. What do you remember of her?

She used to be a right character, didn't she? Used to help out on the flower stall up the market, remember? Everybody round here knew her. You can imagine how she felt about me: 'you're a bad 'un' she used to say and I'd laugh in her face. She kicked me out when you lot left. Acted like she only had one child. You remember Aunty Marilyn?

She's done well for herself. The big house, car, nice husband. They don't want for money that lot. One time I was at King's Cross, I see these two women come towards me. They were walking arm in arm and had their heads thrown back laughing. When you're begging you make quick judgements about people – you get this instinct for who's gonna cough up and who isn't. People who are happy either want to share their good fortune or get rid of you as quickly as possible before you remind them it won't last. So, I went up to them 'please, miss, can you spare some change?' And guess what? – it was Marilyn out on a girly shopping trip with one of her mates. At first she didn't even look at me – just grabbed hold of her bags as though she thought I was gonna mug her. But then she looks up and sees me.

Only she doesn't see me. Looks right through me. Doesn't even realise it's her own sister.

A few years before and it would have been me and her arm-in-arm going round the boutiques.

That's all behind me now. Never look back.

Yard Gal

Rebecca Prichard

Age: Mid-teens to mid-20s
Ethnicity: Black British
Accent: London

PRODUCTION HISTORY

Yard Gal was produced with the Royal Court Theatre and received its first performance there on 7 May 1998, directed by Gemma Bodinetz. The cast was Amelia Lowdell and Sharon Duncan-Brewster, the designer was Es Devlin and the lighting designer was Tina MacHugh. *Yard Gal* was a huge success for Clean Break and for emerging writer Rebecca Prichard, who won the Critics' Circle Award for Most Promising Playwright. The play toured nationally before transferring to the MCC Theater in New York in April 2000. Since then, the play has been produced in Greece, Russia, Amsterdam, Spain and German as well as a further two times in the UK.

CONTEXT FOR PERFORMER

Yard Gal is the story of two teenage girls 'chatting shit, getting fucked, getting high and doing our crimes', as we follow Boo and Marie into the rave scene and girl-gang violence of 1990s East London – but it is also the story of their friendship and devotion to one another. This is a compelling, fast-paced and unforgettable portrait of life on the edge.

In the below monologue, Boo describes the end of a hard-drinking night with their friends. She and Marie are part of a group of girls who hang out in an empty, abandoned flat, but while other people in their group can seem lonely and isolated – especially the troubled Deanne, who features heavily in this monologue – Boo and Marie, in contrast, are anchored by their friendship with one another.

The text has been amended slightly from the original for the purposes of sustaining the monologue form. In the full script, the line, 'Then Deanne went out with a bottle of rum ...' is spoken by Marie; however, for context and storytelling purposes when condensed to a monologue this line can be performed by Boo.

Boo We was on the top floor and each flat had its own balcony. I open
the door and I run out and I look down. Straight away the dark hit me and
I puke up the height make me feel sick. Everyone was laughing at me as I
fell back into the room.

Then Deanne went out with a bottle of rum. She put the bottle on the
ledge of the balcony and she climb up slowly.

She was wearing a tight miniskirt and she hitch it right up. She crouch
on the ledge at first and Sabrina shouted, 'We can see ya knickers.' Then
she raise herself up standing on the ledge. She was swaying unsteady.
The light from the window was lighting up her face and all behind her
was black. And the wind made her scream. She was just screaming going
'YARD GAL WE A RUN TING!' I felt it inside and I said out loud, 'Shit
she gonna kill herself.' Sabrina goes, 'Don't touch her man – you push
her off.' Deanne was laughing going, 'Come up here man it's wicked,' like
she was lovin' it – but I see her fear. She kept her feet still and her body
was stiff underneath her movement. She goes, 'Wine ya body gal' and she
make a few moves like to dance. She lose her balance and put her hand
out to catch herself. I look at Sabrina's eyes and they was wide staring. I
look at Marie and her eyes was closed.

It 'appen so fast. One minute she was laughin' and the next I see her face
look scared. I see her strain as she go back and she put a hand out like we
might catch her and then she was gone. We just had to run out of the flat
or they would question us again when the ambulance come. They said
when they found her she din't have no face. I went back to the home but
I couldn't sleep. I went out on the street to find Marie (I was looking for
you everywhere) but she was gone.

Joanne

Ursula Rani Sarma

Age: Any
Ethnicity: Any
Accent: Any

PRODUCTION HISTORY

Joanne takes the form of five monologues, each written by a different writer: Deborah Bruce, Theresa Ikoko, Laura Lomas, Chinonyerem Odimba and Ursula Rani Sarma. It was first performed at Latitude Festival in July 2015. It then ran at Soho Theatre, London, from 11 August 2015 for three weeks.

It was performed by Tanya Moodie, directed by Róisín McBrinn and designed by Lucy Osborne, with lighting design by Emma Chapman and sound design by Becky Smith.

The production was revived at the Royal Shakespeare Company's Making Mischief Festival in summer 2016. Clean Break commissioned this play to try and highlight the pressure austerity was putting on services for women and the dangerous effect this was having on vulnerable women.

CONTEXT FOR PERFORMANCE

The play charts twenty-four hours in the life of a young woman (Joanne) from the time she leaves prison to the moment she takes her own life. We never meet Joanne but hear from five women who encounter her along the way.

Grace is one of them. She is a police officer, called to a hostel where Joanne has got into a fight. In order to tell us why she decides to help Joanne in her hour of need, Grace tracks back through the pivotal moments that have led her to make that choice. This monologue is her description and memory of one of those moments.

Grace   See me at fifteen then, *grief struck*, throwing some fading
flower down into the pit they buried my Dad in, looking at my mother
sitting there not saying anything, not breathing even, just watching and
thinking, there goes my man ... (*Beat.*) See me thinking he hated flowers,
they made him sneeze. (*Beat, there's a piercing pain to this, he was her
anchor.*)

See me rebelling, smoking, drinking, being a little bitch, five of us
huddled in a corner wearing black, swapping boyfriends, torturing
teachers, trying so hard to be cool it hurt. And then ...

*Beat, the memory has caught her like a wave of nausea, this is raw, too
real, too present.*

In the classroom, schoolyard, lunchroom, there's always one ... and she's
too tall, too fat, too spotty, too flat, too nerdy, too rich, too poor, too
different ... and she's prey for kids like us, in our warm little pack, she's
fair game. This one's name is Patricia, her sin is red hair and a stutter ...
and I don't remember the beginning, probably name calling, mocking,
taunting, then pinching, poking, prodding, hair pulling, lunch times in the
chip shop, pelting her with burgers, pickles, coke cans, and all the time
us laughing, laughing at the sheer adrenalin of it ... of the power of it.
(*Pause, the memory haunts her.*) And then this ... see this ...

*Rawer still, open, alive. Maybe the sparkle of a disco ball, faint like a
memory, echoes of school hall music behind.*

The night Patricia turns up at a school disco in her uniform. We were all
ripped jeans, Radiohead, Doc Martens ... and here was this kid ... just
all fucking wrong. So we got Timmy Franklin to ask her to dance and the
look on her face, unspeakable delight (*she's suddenly this girl, dancing,
her arms around Timmy's neck*), 'he picked me' ... and then once he had
her up there, two of my gang went up behind her and unzipped her skirt,
fell to her ankles, and she just stood there, frozen, long white legs and
white granny pants.

*Long beat, the horror of it, she steps out of the girl's skin and away so
that she can look at her now from the outside.*

The music stopped (*the music stops but the light continues to sparkle*),
silence, laughter, great banshee wails of it and still she just stood there
and then she looked at me and the force of that, what I saw there, the
immensity of it, of what we had done, of what I had let happen, of what I
was part of. The injustice of it rising up in my throat like battery acid, that
taste, chemical, toxic. (*This is the crux of it, what's been eating her ever
since.*)

Beat, stops, breathes.

She hung herself two weeks later, or tried to, her mother rushed her to the hospital but the damage was done. Cerebral anoxia, her brain had been shut off from oxygen for too long and that was it for her, rest of her life in a wheelchair getting her meals through a straw ... and we did that. (*Beat.*) I did that. For a laugh ... (*Beat.*) she was 15 years old.

Red

Anna Reynolds

Age: Mid-20s or older
Ethnicity: Any
Accent: Any

PRODUCTION HISTORY

Red was first performed at the New End Theatre, Hampstead, on 1 April 1994, directed by Fiona Buffini. The cast was Leonora Rogers-Wright and Carrie Thomas. Playwright Anna Reynolds was Clean Break's writer in residence at the time, and the play draws on her own lived experience of the criminal justice system: Reynolds was convicted as a long-term prisoner as a teenager, before her conviction was repealed in her early twenties.

CONTEXT FOR PERFORMANCE

Red follows two women – middle-class Gerda and working-class Kay – who are being held in the same cell during their trial. They appear to be from different worlds, but both have been arrested for murdering their husbands: Kay, in a moment of passion and fury, while Gerda is accused of driving her young lover on to do it for her. Over the course of the play, which is written in a sparse, poetic style, the two women form a tentative friendship and mutual understanding.

When Kay meets Gerda, she is in court for an appeal, but she has already been in prison for some time, making her more knowledgeable and experienced in the intricacies of the justice system than Gerda is. In this monologue, Kay describes her return to prison after her retrial was rejected, and the experience of being a long-term prisoner in a place where many other women are only passing through.

Kay is seemingly a confident character who tries to convey a 'seen it all' attitude, but she is struggling with a lot of inner turmoil, self-recrimination and regret, which the audience can occasionally glimpse.

Kay   The night I came back from court, the screws in reception were like, 'What are you doing back here? Thought you'd get off.'

They put me in Receptions with Lin. Done eighteen years of a life and when she went to get ready to go all her clothes were Seventies throwbacks. Plastic bomber jacket, flared cords. Jammy lipstick and somebody else's shoes. They've lost hers long ago. She gets dressed and somebody starts to laugh. Then it stops because we can all see the future.

That night I never slept at all. I sat watching the dawn break. There was no sun that morning. The door opened and a screw pushed a tray of cold food and a brush inside the cell and slammed the door. I knew it would be like that forever. Going down the gym with people doing two years, and six months. One girl in education doing twenty-eight days because she couldn't pay a fine. I went for her. She was crying, see. 'What if my bloke doesn't wait for me?'

I hit her with a typewriter.

It was the heaviest thing there was. They put me down the block and wouldn't let me have a shower.

Believe me, I've been a cunt to live with. I chased David with a knife once.

House

Somalia Seaton

Age: 50s
Ethnicity: Afro-Caribbean or African
Accent: Nigerian or UK

PRODUCTION HISTORY

House was first performed at the Assembly Box at the Edinburgh Fringe Festival on 4 August 2016, where it ran until 27 August before transferring to the Yard Theatre, London, running from 1 to 17 September. The cast was Rebecca Omogbehin, Shvorne Marks and Michelle Greenidge. *House* was staged in a double bill with *Amongst the Reeds* by Chinonyerem Odimba. Both plays were directed by Róisín McBrinn and designed by Rachael Canning with lighting design by Natasha Chivers and sound design by Becky Smith.

Both plays came out of Clean Break's Emerging Writers Programme, run with support from the Tricycle Theatre (now Kiln Theatre), Bristol Old Vic and the Royal Exchange Theatre, Manchester.

CONTEXT FOR PERFORMANCE

House follows Pat as she returns to her childhood home after a five-year absence to see her sister and reach out to the mother (Mama) who has turned her back on her. Mama is a naturalized British Nigerian with a Nigerian accent – but the speech could also work with a British accent.

Since Pat was a teenager, she has struggled with mental health problems, probably stemming from childhood abuse she suffered, connected to a man in her mother's church. This has led to a chaotic lifestyle, substance abuse and Pat spending some time in prison. She has recently been released and is working hard to get her life back on track – but Mama cannot understand what she has been through, has not visited her in prison and does not want to see her.

This speech occurs late in the play. Pat and Mama have been arguing about the fact that Mama turned her back on Pat after she became unwell.

Mama is a very proud matriarch who has high expectations of her children and who cannot accept her daughter's behaviour as owing to poor mental health and trauma in her past. Mama has been listening up to this point and now she has her say.

Text in brackets should not be spoken.

Mama   Stop talking!
Stop talking now.
32 years of shame, *that's* what you have given me.
Me, your Mother ... me! With all the sacrifices I have made for you ...
and ... and ... you walk back into this house today ... after you let them
lock you up like some type of ... some type of wild animal ... accusing
me of ... of what? What have I done to make you ... [*treat me this way?*]
... there was a storm that day. It rained for a whole week. Floods
everywhere. Trees fell ... people died, and your father couldn't find my
bag, he didn't even know that I had one.
But somehow we made it ... but you refused to come for 19 hours ... you
wouldn't turn ... you wouldn't move ... so they had to cut you out ... and
you turned blue ... and I cried ... and your father cried ... we all cried.
But you ...
Defiant and stubborn. You. Refused to breathe life into your own lungs.
Made us wait until *you* were ready.
But when you cried
we rejoiced ... our firstborn ... alive by some miracle ...
Then ...
they wouldn't let me hold you ... they took you ... so small ... all those
tubes ... we were all so helpless ... all of us ...
And when you came home, you cried every day non-stop for a whole
year, crying crying crying because you wanted to sleep. Crying crying
crying because you wanted to be awake. Everyday!
But when your father would hold you, you would smile a smile so
beautiful, that all the other smiles would feel jealous, and you would fall
sound asleep in his arms ...
... when he died ...
Even at death he was with *you* ...
All these people ... your daughter she is ill, your daughter she has mental
something or other ... you let these people tell you, you have mental
problems. But *I* looked after you, *I* looked after *all* of you, why would you
want to punish me in this way?

Mercy Fine

Shelley Silas

Age: Mid-20s
Ethnicity: Black British mixed race
Accent: Any UK

PRODUCTION HISTORY

Mercy Fine was first performed at the Drum, Birmingham Rep, on 5 October 2005. After running at the Drum, the play toured to York Theatre Royal, Salisbury Playhouse and Southwark Playhouse, as well as various women's prisons. It was directed by Natasha Betteridge and the cast was Lynne Verrall, Louise Bangay, Bindya Solanki and Hazel Holder. The designer was Bernadette Roberts, with lighting by Catriona Silver and sound design by Adrienne Quartly.

Writer Shelley Silas's research included running a creative writing group at HMP East Sutton Park, from May to July 2004, and her play is dedicated to the women she taught there.

CONTEXT FOR PERFORMANCE

When the play begins, Mercy Fine is awaiting her forthcoming release from prison, having been inside over nine years for the murder of her stepfather, Frank. The play cuts between scenes taking place inside the prison, where Mercy and the friends she has made prepare for her release, and monologues in which her mother Jean is addressing the audience.

Mercy's closest friend in prison is Viv, her cellmate; in the first scene, Mercy confides in Viv that she is not looking forward to her release. She is scared to leave the certainty of prison life for an uncertain future. Having gone into prison when she was a teenager, Mercy does not know much about the outside world. She is also afraid to return home, to the place where everything went wrong.

Mercy is a calm, kind person, well-liked by the people around her. Despite being imprisoned for murder, she is not violent and does not get into arguments. She is very gentle with other people and her relationship with Viv is warm and sincere.

In this section, which occurs late in the play, Mercy is again confiding in Viv about how difficult her stepfather was – and how badly he treated both her and her mother, who Mercy was very close to and loves very much.

Mercy   You know, she was the sweetest, most generous. ... She would get up at six, make coffee for him so it was hot when he woke up. She had a bath and put on her make up, because he said he didn't want to look at an ugly cow in the morning or smell her night time smell. She wore thick mascara and painted her lips so they were bright. And she walked quietly around the place, so she didn't disturb him. And I'd listen, and watch, as she walked around her home like it belonged to someone else. Like it belonged to him. Because that's how he used to act. Like he owned the place. Like fuck he did. He used to treat her like shit. Like a dog. And I had to watch. If he didn't like something she cooked for him, he'd throw it in the bin. If we were having dinner or watching TV, and he wanted to have sex, he'd click his fingers at me and I'd have to go outside and wait. And wait. So I'd go down the chip shop, get some chocolate. Keep me warm and wired. And he played music. All the time. That fucking music, made me mad. And his mouth, his mouth said words no one should say, words that no one should hear. He said a white woman needed a white man, not a man like my father. He said I was like washing that hadn't been rinsed out. I was like a stain. A big stain. I told her what he said, and she laughed.

21.23.6.15

Sandrine Uwayo

Age: Any
Ethnicity: Any
Accent: Any

PRODUCTION HISTORY

At the time of publication, Sandrine is a Member of Clean Break's Brazen Programme for young women and attends the Writers' Circle, currently run by Deborah Bruce.

This piece has yet to be performed outside of the Clean Break building and was chosen for its originality and accomplished poetic style.

CONTEXT FOR PERFORMANCE

In the writer's words, the piece is 'about a spiritual journey to heal oneself through passing on wisdom to loved ones.' Sandrine has structured her piece very specifically to reflect the rhythm she wants the piece to have. The use of original words is also a choice.

A Voice   to the adult you I never got to know
to all of you ze, I apologise
the 21 year old boy, the 15-old girl, the 23-year-old boy AND THE boy
who will one day be 11, 13, 17. But right now, is only barely beginning to
comprehend, Understand and ask for me.
TO the 6 OLD YOU.
most of all,
I APOLOGISE.

Here is what I should have said when you came of age
nobody and I mean nobody is entitled to your body
you are   bold,   beautiful,   kind,
miserable,   ugly   mean   scared   suicidal   lonely
strong   you have urgency,
you have LIGHT
                    spirit   resilience   a voice
nobody will ever love you as much as you,
you are frail
Franticly lost   barely keeping your head above the water
but   you,   you are surviving
more and more each day you keep on living
Speak and give testament to the future
Inspire Generations
Legacies
You WILL not be defined by your gender, sexuality, race, background
Above all you are NOT a political weapon.   to use for or against YOU

Scream if you want to
cry when you hurt
give and receive love to your heart's content
advocate for as much or as little as your heart contents
Run fast   slow down   Take in the beauty around you.
                                        be bold.   boundless.
Get lost   but remember to take a torch with you, so you can always
come home to me.
Be Impatient and unsatisfied with life.
Be restless   demand more   BE, HELPLESS   unguarded   defenceless
Be ugly on purpose
Have many, many lovers so you can learn how to love in return
Be hurt
Teach and be taught tough lessons

write prose
Content Shakespeare   Inspire ANGELS to make THE DEVIL ... .
                    SING
Simply come to me at the end of it all. Lay your head on my lap and tell
me your worries AND HURT
i am finally able to give you a home.
ready to listen.

And I and Silence

Naomi Wallace

Age: 25
Ethnicity: White American
Accent: US

PRODUCTION HISTORY

And I and Silence was first performed at the Finborough Theatre on 10 May 2011, directed by Caitlin McLeod. The play was originally commissioned by Clean Break and was produced by Worn Red Theatre and Ben Canning in association with Clean Break and Neil McPherson. The play was initially developed by Lucy Morrison, who co-ran workshops at HMP Morton Hall in 2008 with playwright Naomi Wallace, as part of Naomi's research process for the play.

CONTEXT FOR PERFORMANCE

Set in 1950s segregated America, *And I and Silence* depicts a powerful friendship between Dee, a white American woman, and Jamie, an African American woman. The play is for four performers and alternates, scene-to-scene, between the teenage Jamie and Dee meeting in prison and the older Jamie and Dee struggling to get by on the outside.

In this section, Dee is talking about how, in some ways, things seemed easier when they were in prison and their friendship wasn't as directly disrupted by the racist segregation policies of mid-twentieth-century America.

Young Dee is a lively, smart character who is full of hope – the older Dee is still clever and passionate, but she is more hardened, more affected by life. Despite her newfound freedom, she still does not feel free, and is rapidly losing the hope for a better life that she and Jamie worked so hard to hold onto in prison.

Dee   We were happy when we were inside. Sometimes.

We found a way to meet. Here, we can't go out together. We can't sit together. We can't walk together any more.

'Cause folks on the street see us together, everyone thinks you're my maid. Me, have a maid? How could I ever afford a maid?

We walk down on Oak Street, go into BB-Jigs hardware for a light bulb. The guy who looks like Mr Potato Head's Uncle with a pipe asks and asks how we know each other so we say that really you're not my servant. But he doesn't believe us, so we tell Mr Potato Head's Uncle the truth: that we're both servants. That we're friends. What do we get then?

What do we get? An orange crush bottle flying through the air. Then another 'cross my back. Guts from the butcher in your hair. Doors slamming behind us –

They're not my people.

I wish I could kill people and get away with it.

When we were inside at least our bellies were full.

Permissions Acknowledgements

Little on the inside, © Alice Birch, 2019

[BLANK] © Alice Birch, 2018, by kind permission of Oberon Books Ltd.

Black Crows © Linda Brogan, 2007, by kind permission of Oberon Books Ltd.

Jadan © Danni Brown, 2019

Joanne © Ursula Rani Sarma and Deborah Bruce, 2015, by kind permission of Nick Hern Books.

Didn't Die © Annie Caulfield, 2019

Thick as Thieves © Kath Chandler, 2018, by kind permission of Nick Hern Books.

Spent © Kath Chandler, 2019

Apache Tears © Lin Coghlan, 2019

Head Rot Holiday © Sarah Daniels, 1994

Trainers © Raina Dunne AKA Titch, 2019

Fingertips © Suhayla El-Bushra, 2019

Pests © Vivienne Franzmann, 2014, by kind permission of Nick Hern Books.

Sounds Like an Insult © Vivienne Franzmann, 2019

Blis-ta © Sonya Hale, 2019

Daddycation © Katie Hims, 2019

The Garden Girls from *Holborough: Three Plays* © Jaqueline Holborough, 2006, by kind permission of Oberon Books Ltd.

Killers © Jaqueline Holborough, 2019

FKA Queens © Theresa Ikoko, 2019

Firm © Daisy King, 2019

it felt empty when the heart went at first but it is alright now © Lucy Kirkwood, 2009, by kind permission of Nick Hern Books.

Wicked © Bryony Lavery, 1990

That Almost Unnameable Lust © Rebecca Lenkiewiez, 2010, by kind permission of Nick Hern Books.

Typical Girls © Morgan Lloyd Malcom, 2019

Amazing Amy © Laura Lomas, 2019

Inside a Cloud © Sabrina Mahfouz, 2019

A Bitch Like Me © Natasha Marshall, 2019

Fatal Light and *This Wide Night* © Chloe Moss, 2010, 2008, by kind permission of Nick Hern Books.

Amongst the Reeds © Chinoyerem Odimba, 2016, by kind permission of Nick Hern Books.

Te Awa I Tahuti (The River That Ran Away) © Rena Owen, 2019

Mules © Winsome Pinnock, 1996, by kind permission of Faber and Faber Ltd.

Taken © Winsome Pinnock, 2010, by kind permission of Nick Hern Books.

Yard Girl © Rebecca Pritchard, 1998, by kind permission of Faber and Faber Ltd.

Joanne © Ursula Rani Sarma and Deborah Bruce, 2015, by kind permission of Nick Hern Books.

Red © Anna Reynolds, 2019

House © Somalia Seaton, 2016, by kind permission of Nick Hern Books.

Mercy Fine © Shelley Silas, 2017, by kind permission of Oberon Books Ltd.

21.23.6.15 © Sandrine Uwayo, 2019

And I and Silence © Naomi Wallace, 2019

Permissions Information

Methuen Drama
Bloomsbury Publishing Plc, 50 Bedford Square, London, WC1B 3DP, UK

Nick Hern Books
All rights whatsoever in the following plays are strictly reserved. *Taken* by Winsome Pinnock, *it felt empty when the heart went at first but it is alright now* by Lucy Kirkwood, *Joanne* by Ursula Rani Sarma and Deborah Bruce, *That Almost Unnameable Lust* by Rebecca Lenkiewicz, *Fatal Light* and *This Wide Night* by Chloe Moss, *House* by Somalia Seaton, *Pests* by Vivienne Franzmann, *Amongst the Reeds* by Chinoyerem Odimba, *Thick as Thieves* by Kath Chandler. Requests to reproduce the text in whole or in part should be addressed to Nick Hern Books www.nickhernbooks.co.uk.

Amateur Performing Rights: Applications for performance, including readings and excerpts, by amateurs throughout the world (excluding the United States of America and Canada) should be addressed in the first instance to the Performing Rights Manager, Nick Hern Books, 49a Goldhawk Road, London W12 8QP, tel +44 (0) 20 8749 4953, e-mail rights@nickhernbooks.co.uk except as follows:

Australia: Dominie Drama, 8 Cross Street, Brookvale 2100, fax (2) 9905 5209, e-mail dominie@dominie.com.au

New Zealand: Play Bureau, PO Box 420, New Plymouth, fax (6)753 2150, e-mail play.bureau.nz@xtra.co.nz

Professional Performing Rights: Applications for performance by professionals in any medium and in any language throughout the world (and by amateur and stock companies in the United States of America and Canada) should be addressed to the following agents: for *Taken* by Winsome Pinnock, *it felt empty when the heart went at first but it is alright now* by Lucy Kirkwood, *That Almost Unnameable Lust* by Rebecca Lenkiewicz, *Fatal Light* and *This Wide Night* by Chloe Moss to Casarotto Ramsay at www.casarotto.co.uk, for *House* by Somalia Seaton and *Pests* by Vivienne Franzmann to United Agents www.unitedagents.co.uk, for *Amongst the Reeds* by Chinoyerem Odimba to The Agency www.theagency.co.uk, for *Thick as Thieves* by Kath Chandler to Curtis Brown www.curtisbrown.co.uk, for *Joanne* by Eurula Rani Sarma and Deborah Bruce, please contact both respective agents at www.unitedagents.co.uk and www.casarotto.co.uk.

No performance of any kind may be given unless a licence has been obtained. Applications should be made before rehearsals begin. Publication of this play does not necessarily indicate its availability for performance.

Oberon Books
521 Caledonian Rd, London N7 9RH.

Faber and Faber
https://www.faber.co.uk/permissions.